easy going
locker zu super Noten

Schulaufgaben
von bayerischen Gymnasien
Englisch 6

mit 2 Jahrgangsstufentests

mit Lösungen

DURCHBLICKER
$a^2+b^2=c^2$
Lernstudio Arndt

Vorwort

Liebe Schüler, liebe Eltern,

seit der G8-Reform zur Verkürzung der Schulzeit ist Englisch praxisnäher und lebendiger geworden. Diese

Schulaufgaben von bayerischen Gymnasien

Englisch 6

zeigen, welche Aufgabentypen und welcher Schwierigkeitsgrad im G8-Gymnasium in Bayern verlangt werden. Ein großer Teil der Aufgaben habe ich als Englischlehrerin selber entworfen. Schulaufgaben von Nachhilfeschülern unseres ***Durchblicker Lernstudio Arndt*** bilden die Grundlage der Aufgaben in diesem Buch. Wer diese Schulaufgaben konsequent durcharbeitet, dem sind bessere Noten sicher. Durch Übung kommt jeder Schüler zum Erfolg.

In der 6. Klasse werden zunächst ein Jahrgangsstufentest, dann vier Schulaufgaben geschrieben. Oft heißen diese dann „Großer Leistungstest“. Im vorliegenden Band finden sich **zwei Jahrgangsstufentests** (2013 und 2012), die zu Beginn des Schuljahres geschrieben werden, sowie pro Schulaufgabe jeweils zwei Prüfungen. Die acht hier gestellten Schulaufgaben mit Lösungen entsprechen dem hohen Niveau aus Gymnasien in Bayern, die das

Schülerbuch Green Line New 2

im Unterricht verwenden und basieren auf tatsächlich gestellten Aufgaben.

Als Schüler kennst du ***Vocabulary*** mit Übungen zu Vokabeln und ***Grammar*** mit Übungen zur Grammatik. ***Speaking*** lernst du zum Training der Sprachfertigkeit. ***Writing*** übst du durch ***Dictation*** und schulst das Schreiben mit Diktatübungen. ***Dialogue*** und ***Mediation*** dient zur Übersetzung ins Englische. ***Listening Comprehension*** verbessert das Hörverstehen.

Mit diesem Band kannst du Schritt für Schritt alle Schulaufgaben durcharbeiten, bis du fit bist für die nächste Schulaufgabe. Wenn der Lehrer eine Schulaufgabe ankündigt, sagt er z.B. von Unit 1 bis einschließlich Unit 2, dann solltest du die entsprechenden Schulaufgaben üben. Versuche die Aufgaben selbstständig zu lösen wie in einer richtigen Schulaufgabe. Gibt es einen Hörtext im Lösungsteil, lass dir den Text zweimal vorlesen. Vergleiche deine Lösungen mit den Lösungen der Schulaufgaben und korrigiere dich selbst. Wenn sich die Fehler häufen, dann musst du verstärkt Vokabeln lernen oder in der Grammatik oder im Schülerbuch noch einmal die Kapitel, um die es geht, wiederholen.

Mein Ziel ist es, die Motivation und Kreativität aller Schüler beim Lösen von Schulaufgaben in Englisch zu fördern. Dazu biete ich die **ausführliche Lösung** der Aufgabenstellung an.

Viel Spaß beim Lösen der Schulaufgaben

Deine und Ihre Englischtrainerin Monika Arndt

Monika Arndt (Dipl.-Übersetzerin), veröffentlichte als Buchautorin Ernährungsbücher für Kinder in den Verlagen dtv und Ravensburger. **Das Baby-Kochbuch**, **Wie Kinder fit und gesund bleiben** und **Das Ravensburger Kochbuch für Kinder** mit Bildern von Ali Mitgutsch.
Zuvor hat Monika Arndt in verschiedenen Redaktionen gearbeitet, z.B. über zehn Jahre in der Redaktion des Schulfernsehheftes beim Bayerischen Schulfernsehen. Beim Stark-Verlag hat sie über Produktion und Inhalt von Lernhilfen Erfahrungen gesammelt, geeignete Lehrer gesucht und die Bücher als Lektorin redigiert.
Sie unterrichtet Englisch und Französisch im ***Durchblicker Lernstudio Arndt***.

Wir danken Frau Petra Nowak-Walsh, die als Lektorin und Dolmetscherin den Band mit Tipps und Hinweisen ergänzt hat.
Titelbild: Heinrich Schmid, Überlingen am Ried / Singen am Hohentwiel
www.durchblicker.org

ISBN **978-3-00-034521-0**

9 783000 345210

Part I: Listening Comprehension — 20 BE

Part A

1. Fill in the gap and tick (✓) the correct answer. (2 BE)

Tiger is ______ years old and he is
❑ grey, brown and white with long hair.
❑ red, grey and brown with short hair.
❑ white, grey and black with long hair.
❑ white, brown and grey with short hair.

2. Tiger's family. Fill in people's names and ages. (4 BE)

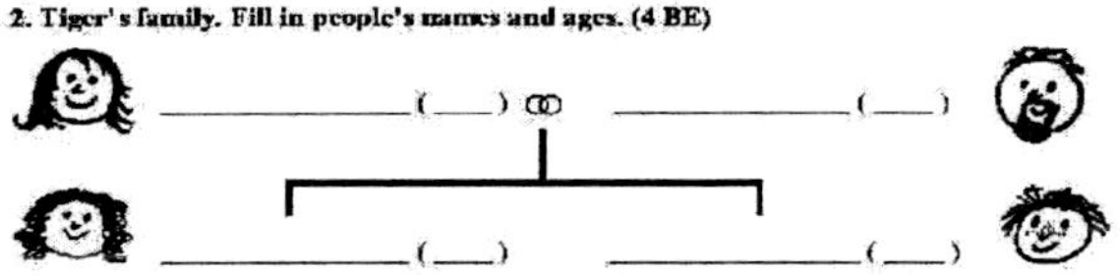

3. Find the correct pairs. Put the correct number in the box. (4 BE)

Polly loves ☐
Tiger loves ☐
Sally loves ☐
Harry loves ☐

1. walking in the park.
2. Tiger's presents.
3. Polly more.
4. catching fish.
5. playing tricks.
6. being in the bathroom.

Part B

4. True or false? (6 BE)

	True	False
Tiger spent[1] the night in the street in front of the garden.	❑	❑
He likes to bring his family what he caught.	❑	❑
He came home to show Polly his mouse.	❑	❑
He got into the house through a door for cats.	❑	❑
On Sunday morning he put a mouse into Harry's bedside table.	❑	❑
Susan got up and shouted at Tiger.	❑	❑

[1] spend – spent: verbringen

Part C

5. What happened to the mouse? Tick the two correct answers. (2 BE)

❑ Tiger didn't eat it.
❑ Polly ate it.
❑ Harry took it outside.
❑ It ran into the bathroom.

6. Why is Tiger angry[2] with Polly? Tick the two correct answers. (2 BE)

❑ She's too stupid to open doors.
❑ She doesn't do anything but still gets food.
❑ She doesn't bring him presents.
❑ She can sleep in Chris's bed.

BE

Part II: Use of English — 16 BE

Katie is staying with a German family for a few weeks. This is her first e-mail home to her parents in England. Read the e-mail and tick what is right ✓. Only one of the three is correct.

Hi everyone,

how are you? I'm fine, and I'm having a great time with my German family, the Lamberts, Mr and Mrs Lambert, Thomas and my pen friend Lisa. (❑ They're / ❑ Their / ❑ There're) very, very nice. Mrs Lambert's English is perfect because she (❑ speaks English in her job every day. / ❑ speaks every day English in her job. / ❑ speaks in her job English every day.)

The (❑ Lambert's house / ❑ Lamberts' house / ❑ house from the Lamberts) is really big, with a wonderful garden around it. And (❑ it has / ❑ it gives / ❑ there is) an outdoor pool just half a mile away, so we (❑ can go to swimming / ❑ can go swimming / ❑ can went swimming) every day. Thomas is very nice; he is Lisa's brother, and it was his fifteenth birthday last week. A lot of his friends (❑ did come / ❑ came / ❑ were come) and they had a party until late at night, and then a neighbour called the police because their music (❑ is / ❑ was / ❑ were) so loud. They had a big birthday cake, too, but they (❑ didn't ate / ❑ can't ate / ❑ didn't eat) it because Lisa's little cat got it first and ate all the cream[3] on it; she looked so funny with the cream all over her face. Thomas was not so happy about this, of course.

[3] cream: Sahne

Last Saturday Lisa and I
❑ went shopping
❑ go shopping
❑ did go shopping
in the city. But it wasn't a good idea:

❑ it were
❑ they were
❑ there were
thousands of people. I didn't get the Coldplay CD, but Lisa is going to download it for me so I
❑ mustn't look
❑ don't must look
❑ needn't look
for it in the city again. Lisa
❑ always buys
❑ does always buy
❑ is always buying
her music online: I didn't know how easy that is. And it
❑ costs not
❑ doesn't cost
❑ don't costs
more than in the shop (don't worry, Mum, we aren't doing anything illegal). What about my brother's Maths test?

❑ Does Tim wrote
❑ Did Tim write
❑ Was Tim write
it yesterday? Was it good? If not, I guess it's because he
❑ never does
❑ doesn't never make
❑ never makes
his homework. Did you know that he always copies it from his friends at school? Don't tell him that I told you! Well, it's getting late now (it's almost
❑ fifteen to ten)
❑ quarter to twenty-two)
❑ quarter to ten)
and I guess I must get some sleep now.

Write back soon.

Katie

Part III: Text Production 20 BE

You're on holiday in London with your family. In Greenwich Park, you meet a group of pupils – in school uniforms! You want to know more about schools in Britain, so you start talking to one of them, Chris. **Complete the dialogue.**

You: Hi, can I ask you a question?

C.: Yes, of course. What do you want to know?

You: I'm from Germany, and we haven't got school uniforms at our schools. What about you? ______________________ every day?

C.: Yes, we do. At school, we ______________________ jeans. Some of my friends think that our uniforms are OK, but I ______________________ ☹ because ______________________.

You: I understand. Oh, sorry, I forgot to tell you my name. I'm ______________________. ______________________?

C.: I'm Chris. Have you got any other questions?

You: My English teacher always tells us that there is "assembly" at British schools. What's that?

C.: ______________________
____

You: That must be ______________________! Are you in any club or group at your school?

C.: **[2 activities at school]** ______________________
____

You: And what do you usually do at the weekend? **[2 activities]**

C.: ______________________
____
But last weekend **[2 activities]** ______________________
____
You are on holiday in London, aren't you? Are you staying in a hotel?

You: Yes, we are. Our hotel is great because **[2 things you like about it]** ______________________
____

C.: And what ______________________ yesterday?

You: We ______________________ a typical London bus and then we ______________________ the British Museum. And tomorrow, we... – oh, that's dad calling me, I must go now. ______________________?

C.: Of course. My address is "c.parker@oops.com".

You: Great – I'm going to write soon. Bye – and thank you!

______ BE

Total: ______ BE

Lösung: Jahrgangsstufentest Englisch 6

I. Listening Comprehension

Part A *(2x vorlesen)*

Miaow, my name is Tiger and I'm a funny cat. I'm eight years old, I'm grey, brown and white with short hair and I live in Newcastle, in England. Me and my family, we don't live in the city centre, but in a part outside. There we have a big garden with many trees and lovely birds and – mmmh… – lots of mice. But I'm going to tell you about that later. Of course, I'm not alone. I've got a nice family – well, they're nice most of the time, but sometimes they're really terrible. Harry and Susan are my big bosses – or they think they are. Harry is 40 and Susan is 38. They've got two children: Chris, 14, and Sally, 13. Chris is OK, but Sally is really nice. I must say I love her because she lets me sleep in her bed and gives me milk, my favourite drink. And she's never angry when I play tricks. She even says I'm a good boy when I bring home presents. But this is quite another story and I'll come to it later, when I tell you about the mouse. Before, I must tell you about Polly. She lives in my family, too, and she is a black cat with really long hair. Polly thinks she is very beautiful and is often in the bathroom. Sometimes I have the feeling that Harry likes her more than me because she's always nice, does what he says and never puts presents into his bedroom.

Part B *(2x vorlesen)*

Now let me tell you about my tricks. Last week, for example, I spent the night outside in our garden and in the park across the street. I was very busy that night and caught a little snake, a bird and a mouse. Normally, when I catch something, I don't kill it but take it home to show it to my family, but at six o'clock on Sunday morning Harry and Susan were still sleeping and they didn't hear me miaow under their bedroom window with the mouse in my mouth. So I went into the house – there is a little door for me and I can go in and out whenever I like – and went up to their bedroom. Their door was shut, but this wasn't a problem because I can open doors. That's one of my favourite tricks. Well, when I was inside their bedroom, I started to miaow louder, but they didn't look at me and didn't get up. So I went up to Susan's bed, got in and put the mouse next to her ear. Well, this trick did the job: Susan jumped out of the bed: "Harry, Harry, wake up, there's a mouse in our bed."

Part C *(2x vorlesen)*

Harry got up, too, threw me out of the bedroom and put me into the bathroom. Then he caught my mouse and put it outside. That made me really angry. How can he be so unfair? I'm nice and bring him lovely presents and he throws me out of his room and doesn't let me eat my mouse. But I was lucky because Sally gave me something else to eat. And she gave me some milk, too. But that day, I was a little angry with Sally because she gave Polly, the stupid cat, some food, too, and she never brings home presents for Chris and Sally! And Chris even let her sleep in his bed the next day. Just because she doesn't open doors! Sometimes I really don't understand my family.

I. Listening Comprehension

Part A

1. Fill in the correct gap and tick the correct answer (2 BE)

Tiger is *eight* years old and he is *white, brown and grey with short hair.*

2. Tiger's family. Fill in people's names and ages (4 BE)

Harry (40, Susan (38), Chris (14), Sally (13)

3. Find the correct pairs. Put the correct number in the box (4 BE)

6, 5, 2, 3

Part B

4. True or false? (6 BE)

a) false b) *true* c) false d) *true* e) false f) false

Part C

5. What happened to the mouse? Tick the two correct answers (2 BE)

a) c)

6. Why is tiger angry with Polly? Tick the two correct answers (2 BE)

b) d)

____/20

Part II: Use of English

...***They're*** very, very nice.	Personalpronomen, Formen von *to be*; Unterscheidung der Homophone *there / they're / their*
...She ***speaks English in her job every day.***	Wortstellung im Aussagesatz (Ort vor Zeit)
...The ***Lamberts' house*** is really big...	Gebrauch des Genitivs
...And ***there is*** an outdoor pool...	vorausweisendes *there;* ***false friends***
..., so we ***can go swimming*** every day...	Gebrauch des Hilfsverbs *can;* ***false friends***
... A lot of friends ***came*** and...	Gebrauch des ***Simple past***
...their music ***was*** so loud...	Gebrauch des *to be* im ***Simple past***
...they ***didn't eat*** it...	Verneinung von Vollverben im ***Simple past***
...Lisa and I ***went shopping*** in the city.	Gebrauch des ***Simple past***
...***there were*** thousands of people...	vorausweisendes *there* mit Verb im ***Simple past***
...I ***needn't look*** for it in the city again...	Gebrauch des Hilfsverbs *needn't*
...Lisa ***always buys*** her music online...	***Simple present vs. Present progressive;*** Stellung von Adverbien
...And it ***doesn't cost*** more than in the shop.	Verneinung von Vollverben
...***Did Tim write*** it yesterday?	Frage im ***Simple past***
...he ***never does*** his homework.	Kollokation; Verneinung mit *never*
...(it's almost ***quarter to ten***) ...	Uhrzeit

Tipps und Hinweise
o Ein *-s* wird ohne Apostroph angehängt, wenn es eine Mehrzahl (Plural) bezeichnet.
Beim Genitiv brauchst du ein Apostroph mit *-s* für Singular und nur ein Apostroph für Plural.
Ausnahme: Wörter, die keinen *-s* Plural haben, bekommen im Genitiv auch Apostroph mit *-s*.
o Bei den meisten **Fragewörtern** musst du mit dem Hilfsverb ***do*** umschreiben. Bei ***who*** und ***what*** musst du aufpassen, ob das Fragewort selbst das Subjekt des Satzes ist oder das Objekt. Ist ***who*** oder ***what*** selbst das Subjekt, wird das Hilfverb ***do*** nicht verwendet.
o Bei **regelmäßigen Verben** wird das ***Simple past*** mit ***-ed*** gemacht. Aber es gibt viele unregelmäßige Verben, bei denen du die einzelnen Formen lernen musst!
Eine Frage stellt man mit ***did*** und man verneint mit ***didn't.***

____/16

Part III: Text Production

...*Do you have to wear them* every day?

...we *are not allowed to wear* jeans.

...I *don't like them* because *I think that everyone should be allowed to dress like they want.*

... I'm *Alexander from Germany. What's your name?*

...*That means that all the pupils at the school have to meet with their teachers and the director before class.*

...That must be *annoying*!

...**[2 activities at school]** *Yes, I play soccer and I swim in the school team.*

...**[2 activities]** *I meet my friends and I play soccer.*

...**[2 activities]** *I 've made a trip with my family to a lake and we did some kajaking.*

...**[2 things you like about it]** *the food is really delicious and we have a huge swimming pool.*

... and what *did you do* yesterday?

...We *drove with* a typical London bus and then we *visited* the British Museum...

...*Can you give me your address?*

____/20

Total ____/56

Tipps und Hinweise
Hier musst du gut aufpassen, ob du das ***Simple present*** oder das ***Present progressive*** verwenden sollst. Denke daran: Das ***Present simple*** nimmst du bei gewohnheitsmäßigen Handlungen sowie für aufeinander folgende Handlungen (auch plötzliche). Vergiss dann bei ***he / she / it*** das *-s* nicht! Das ***Present progressive*** brauchst du, wenn etwas gerade und / oder vorübergehend geschieht.

Part I: Listening Comprehension **20 BE**

Back to school

Part A:

1. *Fill in the correct numbers.* (2 BE)

It's the first day after the holidays: Tuesday _______ September, ☐:☐☐ in the morning.

2. Where in London is Stratford School? *Tick the correct answer.* (1 BE)

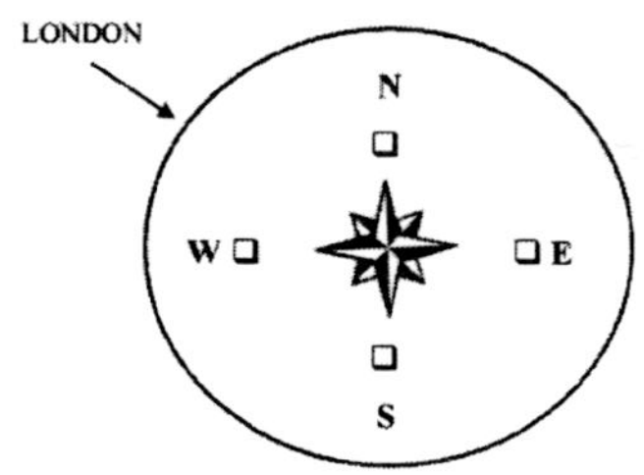

3. Right or wrong? *Tick the correct answer.* (3 BE)

	right	wrong
The head teacher[1] welcomes the pupils in the gym.	❑	❑
The two visitors are gold medal winners.	❑	❑
One of them went to Singapore with some of the children.	❑	❑

4. *Match (→) the teachers with their jobs.* (4 BE)

	English teacher
a) Mrs Green	French teacher
b) Mrs Coe	Head teacher
c) Mr Chevin	Geography teacher
d) Mr Roberts	Sports teacher
	Maths teacher

[1] head teacher: *Schulleiter(in)*

Part B:

5. Who gave the Olympic Games to London? *Tick the correct answer.* (1 BE)

❑ ICE ❑ EOC
❑ IOC ❑ CEO

6. When did London have the Olympic Games before 2012? (2 BE)

- ____________________
- ____________________

7. How many sportspeople took part in the Games? (1 BE)

____

8. *Tick the two correct answers.* (2 BE)

❑ Boys and girls liked the same sports best.
❑ The boys' favourite sports were games like football, handball etc.
❑ The girls had no special favourites.
❑ Some of them found the tennis games interesting.

Part C:

9. What are the main ideas behind the project[2]? *Tick the two correct answers.* (2 BE)

❑ to make pupils fitter
❑ to have international football matches
❑ to invite American and German teachers to competitions[3] at Stratford School
❑ to have more sports lessons at school

10. When is the new football lesson? *Tick the correct answers.* (2 BE)

❑ Tuesday ❑ 1:30
❑ Wednesday ❑ 2:30
❑ Thursday ❑ 3:30

BE

[2] project: *Vorhaben, Projekt*
[3] competition: *Wettbewerb*

Part II: Use of English — 18 BE

Read the following text and tick what is right ☑. Only one of the three is correct.

I am Simon, the Sock. It's
- ☐ quarter past seven
- ☐ quarter behind seven
- ☐ fiveteen after seven

and I
- ☐ ly
- ☐ am lying
- ☐ lie

here in the drawer[4].
- ☐ Who
- ☐ Where
- ☐ How

does Peter want to take today? I hate mornings because you never know: is it you or another pair of socks? Suddenly Peter
- ☐ opened
- ☐ is opening
- ☐ opens

the drawer and this time
- ☐ I have not luck:
- ☐ I'm not lucky:
- ☐ I don't be lucky:

He
- ☐ chose
- ☐ chooses
- ☐ is choosing

me and puts me on. Well, OK, his feet[5] are clean, but this
- ☐ change
- ☐ can changes
- ☐ can change

very fast when they
- ☐ mustn't leave[6]
- ☐ don't must leave
- ☐ needn't to leave

the boots for the rest of the day. And it's winter, so Peter
- ☐ wears every day the same boots.
- ☐ wears the same boots every day.
- ☐ does every day wear the same boots.

Downstairs in the kitchen, Max,
- ☐ the dog of Peter,
- ☐ the dog from Peter,
- ☐ Peter's dog,

comes to say hello and sits on me. Ugh, I hate
- ☐ these silly dog.
- ☐ this silly dog.
- ☐ that silly dogs.

Sometimes, he takes me and hides me. In the kitchen Peter
- ☐ doesn't watch out
- ☐ don't watch out
- ☐ watches not out

and runs into
- ☐ a bottle of milk.
- ☐ a bottle full milk.
- ☐ a bottle milk.

Now
- ☐ their's
- ☐ theirs
- ☐ there's

milk on the floor and he puts his left foot into it. Now I'm wet! Peter could[7] take
- ☐ every new socks
- ☐ some new socks
- ☐ a new socks

– he has got
- ☐ so many of them
- ☐ so much of them
- ☐ so lots of them

– but he's late, as usual, so I start my day wet in a pair of boots.
- ☐ Why took Peter me?
- ☐ Why did Peter took me?
- ☐ Why did Peter take me?

I'm not happy at all. I know
- ☐ it's going to be a terrible day.
- ☐ it's go to being a terrible day.
- ☐ it's going be a terrible day.

[4] drawer: *Schublade* – [5] feet: *Füße* – [6] leave: *verlassen* – [7] could: *könnte*

BE

Part III: Mediation — 17 BE

Potter's Toy Museum

Potter's Toy Museum is in two neighbouring houses in the centre of London. The rooms are small and the place is full of the atmosphere of childhood. Every room is filled with wonderful things and there are new surprises everywhere.

Room 1:	card and table games
Room 2:	models (toy cars, trains, ships etc.)
Room 3:	everything that flies (model planes, balloons, kites etc.)
Room 4:	dolls from around the world ("Barbie" dolls, speaking dolls etc.)
Room 5:	the "Animal Paradise": teddy bears and others
Room 6:	picture books from Europe
Room 7:	dolls' houses and clothes
Room 8:	board games and dominoes
Ground floor:	Potter's Toyshop

Location:
18 Scala Street
London W1T 2HL
phone: 020 9637 2458
info@potterstoymuseum.com
www.potterstoymuseum.com

Opening Hours:
Monday to Saturday
10 a.m. – 5 p.m.
Last entry to museum: 4.30pm
Closed Bank Holidays

How to get there:
By Underground:
Goodge Street, Warren Street,
Euston Square,
Tottenham Court Road

Admission:
Adults: £7.95
Children under 14: £3.95
Family group (2 adults and up to four children): £19.95

Der zwölfjährige Tim ist mit seinen Eltern und seiner jüngeren Schwester zu Besuch in London. Im Internet hat er die Website dieses Museums gefunden. Seine Schwester Lisa, die noch kein Englisch kann, möchte nun wissen, was er da entdeckt hat. Er erklärt es ihr **auf Deutsch**.

Lisa: Was hast du da gefunden? Ist das ein Laden, wo wir was einkaufen können?

Nein, es ist ein Museum, wo man ______________ sehen kann. Einen Laden haben sie aber auch dabei.

Tim (1 BE)

Lisa: Cool, und was haben die alles? Gibt es interessante Sachen zu sehen?

Ja. Die schreiben hier, im ersten Raum gibt es ______________ ______________, und im zweiten Raum ______________ ______________.

Tim (2 BE)

Lisa: Haben die auch Puppen und Puppensachen?

Ja, Puppen haben sie in Raum ________ und dazu passend haben sie in einem anderen Raum ______________ ______________ ______________.

Tim (2 BE)

Lisa: Und was noch?

______________ ______________ ______________ ______________.

Tim (nennt zwei noch nicht genannte Dinge) (2 BE)

Lisa: Toll, können wir da am Wochenende hin?

Na ja, das ginge ______________ ______________, aber nicht ______________, da haben sie nicht offen.

Tim (2 BE)

Nach dem Museumsbesuch ist es schon ziemlich spät geworden und Tims Schwester hat ihre Fahrkarte verloren. Tim ruft Mrs Simpson, die Vermieterin ihrer Frühstückspension, an. Mrs Simpson spricht nur **Englisch**.

Mrs Simpson: Hello.

Hi, Mrs Simpson, this is Tim. ______________ ______________

Tim fragt, ob er seine Eltern sprechen kann. (1 BE)

Mrs Simpson: I'm sorry, they went out 5 minutes ago.

______________ ______________

Tim fragt, wo sie hingegangen sind. (1 BE)

Mrs Simpson: Sorry, I don't know. What's the problem, Tim?

______________ ______________ ______________

Tim erklärt das Problem und fragt, ob sie sie beide abholen kann. (2 BE)

Mrs Simpson: Yes, of course.

______________ ______________ ______________

Tim sagt ihr, dass er das echt toll findet, denn sie haben so viel im Museum gekauft, dass sie das alles kaum schleppen können. (3 BE)

Mrs Simpson: Where are you now?

______________ ______________

Tim sagt, dass sie vor dem Museum auf sie warten. (1 BE)

Mrs Simpson: Ok, see you in a minute.

BE
Total: BE

Lösung: Jahrgangsstufentest Englisch 6

Part I: Listening Comprehension

Part A *(2x vorlesen)*

It's the first day after the holidays: Tuesday 4th September, 8:45 in the morning.
At Stratford School in East London the pupils are starting to arrive. The school doors are closed, everyone is outside talking. The teachers are there, too. What is going on? Why can't they go in? The head teacher, Mrs Coe, comes out of a door at the side of the school. She is really smiling. Is she so happy to see them? She doesn't open the doors. What is she doing? She says, "Boys and girls, welcome back! We have a surprise for you. I want to start this school year in the gym. Please go there with your teachers."
Mrs Green, the Maths teacher, and Mr Chevin, the French teacher, take all the new pupils with them and show them the way. They're last.
In the gym at the back of the school Mr Roberts and Mrs Black, the Sports teachers, are waiting. There are two men with them. One is a very famous sportsman. All the pupils know this man. He won two gold medals in the summer. The other man is not a sportsman but they know him as a sports-reporter from TV. And some of the boys and girls know him better because they went on a very special trip to Singapore with him. The pupils are all very happy to see the two men. Now they know why the head teacher is so excited. They are, too.

Part B *(2x vorlesen)*

The sports-reporter speaks to them:
"Hello, boys and girls. Thanks for the invitation! I'm here today to say thank you. Some of you went to the IOC in Singapore with us and helped us to bring the Olympic Games to London. You worked very hard and you were very good. And London is the first city to have the games three times – in 1908, 1948 and this summer. The Olympic Games were great. It was a fantastic summer! Did you all get your free tickets? Who were your favourites? What sport did you like best? 70,000 sportspeople from all over the world were here. Did you meet any of them?"
Lots of pupils start to answer. They all want to talk to the visitors and tell them about their time at the Olympic Games and who they saw and what they liked. Some say they liked the swimming and some the running or the tennis. The girls all liked the horse riding competitions but the boys liked the team games best. But no one can understand a word, because everyone is talking at the same time! The head teacher Mrs Coe puts up her hand:
"Shush! School, our visitors are here for the day. You can tell them all about your visits to the Games when they come into your class. But now they want to talk to all of you about sport and what you can do all year and how you can get fit and have fun. They have something exciting to tell you, so listen!"
No problem, the pupils stop talking.

Part C *(2x vorlesen)*

Now the famous sportsman can tell everyone about their plan:
"Boys and girls, you helped us all and now we want to help you. We are starting a competition this year with boys and girls in schools here and in America and Germany. We want you to do

more sports at school and after school. We want you to be fit, be active and win prizes. Look at the posters Mr Roberts and Mrs Black, your Sport teachers, have put up all over the school. Lots of sports, lots of schools. And two new Sport teachers, my friend here and I. My sports class is Tuesday at 3:30 here in the gym. Thursdays, it's football with my old friend here at 1:30 out on the sports ground. You all know him from TV, but let me tell you, he's a brilliant football player. The next Olympics are in four years. Let's get fit!"
On the way back to their classrooms the boys and girls are all talking about the new plans. What a start to the school year! It's going to be great!

I. Listening Comprehension

Back to school

Part A

1. Fill in the correct numbers (2 BE)

It's the first day after holidays: Tuesday *4th* September, *8:45* in the morning.

2. Where in London is Stratford School? Tick the correct answer (1 BE)

N o E *x* S o W o

3. Right or wrong? Tick the correct answer (3 BE)

	right	wrong
The head teacher[1] welcomes the pupils in the gym.	o	*x*
The two visitors are gold medal winners	o	*x*
One of them went to Singapore with some of the children.	*x*	o

4. Match the teachers with their jobs (4 BE)

a) Mrs Green	*Maths teacher*
b) Mrs Coe	*Head teacher*
c) Mr Chevin	*French teacher*
d) Mr Roberts	*Sports teacher*

Part B

5. Who gave the Olympic Games to London? Tick the correct answer (1 BE)

o	ICE	o	EOC
x	IOC	o	CEO

6. When did London have the Olympic Games before 2012? (2 BE)

1908 1948

7. How many sportspeople took part in the Games? (1 BE)

70,000

8. Tick the <u>two</u> correct answers (2 BE)

o Boys and girls liked the same sports best.

x The boys' favourite sports were games like football, handball etc.
o The girls had no special favourites.
x Some of them found the tennis games interesting.

Part C

9. What are the main ideas behind the project? Tick the <u>two</u> correct answers (2 BE)
x to make pupils fitter
o to have international football matches
o to invite American and German teachers to competitions (Wettbewerb) at Stratford School
x to have more sports lessons at school

10. When is the new football lesson? Tick the correct answer (2 BE)

o Tuesday	*x* 1:30
o Wednesday	o 2:30
x Thursday	o 3:30

____/20

Part II: Use of English

Read the following text and tick what is right. Only one of the three is correct.

I am Simon, the Sock. It's	*x* quarter past seven	and I	o ly
	o quarter behind seven		*x* am lying
	o quarter after seven		o lie

here in the drawer	*x* Who	does Peter want to take today? I hate mornings because
	o Where	
	o How	

you never know: is it you or another pair of socks? Suddenly Peter	o opened	
	o is opening	the drawer
	x opens	

	o I have not luck:		o chose	
and this time	*x* I'm not lucky:	He	*x* chooses	me and puts me on. Well, OK,
	o I don't be lucky:		o is choosing	

his feet (Füße) are clean, but this	o change		*x* mustn't leave
	o can changes	very fast when they	o don't must leave
	x can change		o needn't to leave

the boots for the rest of the day. It's winter, so Peter	o wears every day the same boots.
	x wears the same boots every day.
	o does every day wear the same boots.

Downstairs in the kitchen, Max, o the dog of Peter, comes to say hello and sits on me.
o the dog from Peter,
x Peter's dog,

Ugh, I hate o these silly dogs. Sometimes, he takes me and hides me. In the kitchen
x this silly dog.
o that silly dogs.

Peter *x* doesn't watch out and runs into *x* a bottle of milk. Now o their's milk
o don't watch out o a bottle full milk. o theirs
o watches not out o a bottle milk. *x* there's

on the floor and puts his left foot into it. Now I'm wet! Peter could take
o every new socks
o some new socks
x a new socks

– he has got *x* so many of them – but he's late, as usual, so I start my day wet in a pair of boots.
o so much of them
o so lots of them

o Why took Peter me? I'm not happy at all. I know *x* it's going to be a terrible day.
o Why did Peter took me? o it's going to being a terrible day.
x Why did Peter take me? o it's going be a terrible day.

____/18

Part III: Mediation

1 Spielzeug / Spielwaren
2a Karten- und Tischspiele / Gesellschaftsspiele
2b Spielzeugautos, -schiffe und -eisenbahnen / Modellspielzeug
3a vier
3b Puppenhäuser und Puppenkleider
4 zwei der folgenden Beispiele: *Modellflugzeuge, Ballons, Drachen („alles, was fliegt"), Teddybären, Stofftiere, Bilderbücher aus ganz Europa / aus verschiedenen Ländern (nicht: über Europa), Brettspiele Dominosteine*
5 am Samstag (Zeitangabe nicht nötig)
5b am Sonntag
6 Can I speak to my parents, please?
7 Where did they go? / Do you know where they went?
8 My sister lost her (bus / tube) ticket. Can you come and pick us up / fetch us, Mrs Simpson?
9 That's cool. We bought so much at the museum that we can't carry it all.
10 We're waiting outside / in front of the museum.

____/17

1. Schulaufgabe aus dem Englischen

Name: ________________________________

Stoff: Unit 1–2

I. Grammar

1. Fill in the correct preposition

______ the afternoon my dad is often away ______ business. He usually works ______ home, sometimes also ______ night or ______weekends. But ______ September he was ______ holiday ______ the seaside. When he came home ______ September 30th, he saw a lot of children ______ the street ______ front of our house. They were queuing up ______ pairs. What on earth were they doing there?

2. Simple past or Past progressive?

Simon and Robert _______________ (play) football while Becky and Sarah ________________ (watch) them. The two boys ________________ (still, play) when it ________________ (start) to rain. So they all ______________ (go) home. When Robert ________________ (arrive), his Mum ________________ (wait) for him. Mrs Croft: "Hi Robert! Can you imagine? I ______________ (fall) off my bike and ________________ (break) my arm!" Robert: "Oh, I´m really sorry, Mum!"

3. Make comparisons

1. Ben Nevis is the ________________ (high) mountain. Mount Everest is ________________ (high) than Ben Nevis. 2. For me Harry Potter is one of ________________ (interesting) books in the world. My sister thinks comics are ____________________ (funny) books.

3. This English test was ______________________ (difficult) of all. No, I think it was _________________ (easy) the last. A Math test is __________________ (bad) a terrible cold. But one week in bed is _________________ (bad) of all.

4. In Robin Hood's time the King was a ________________ (cruel) man. Some of his sheriffs were ________________ (cruel) him. The Sheriff of Nottingham was ________________ (cruel) of them all.

5. New York is a modern city. Munich is ________________ (big) New York, but it is ________________ (big) Augsburg.

6. Sailing is ________________ (dangerous) jogging, rock climbing is ________________ (dangerous) sport of the three.

4. Complete the sentences with question tags

a) You're interested in football, ________________________________?

b) Dave has got a car, ____________________________ ?

c) John wasn't in the theatre last year, ________________________________?

d) They didn't show "Cats", ___________________________?

e) Scott and Dave weren't there yesterday, ________________________?

5. Ask for the underlined words

a) Sabrina was telling a joke when the teacher came in.

____

b) The boy grabbed her bag.

____

c) Robin Hood protected the poor peasants.

____

d) The peasants liked Robin Hood very much.

____

e) The man was talking to the visitors.

____

f) He arrived at home at ten o'clock.

____

II. Translation

1. Nächste Woche spiele ich auf der Bühne in der Schulhalle (Theater).

____

2. Sandra gewann das Tennisspiel, nicht wahr?

____

3. Während die Schüler einen Test schrieben, war ihre Lehrerin verschwunden.

____

____

4. Als die Lehrerin in das Klassenzimmer zurück rannte, ließ sie (plötzlich) ihre Schultasche fallen.

____

____

5. Ein Schüler hinter ihr sah die Schultasche zu spät und stolperte über sie.

____

____

III. Dialogue

Fill in the gaps. Be careful with the verb forms. Sometimes you need to fill in more than one word

One day in her lunch break, Sally ________________ (to read) the notices at the activity board when she ________________ (to hear) a voice behind her. She ________________ (to turn) round and ________________ (to see) a boy.

Peter: Hi, I'm Peter. You're the new girl from Scotland, ________________? What's your name?

Sally: Hello, nice to meet you. Do you like the activities at our school?

Peter: I ________________ (beitreten) the pet club. I like animals. What about you?

Sally: I'm sorry. I can't because I'm ________________ (allergisch gegen) cats. They ________________ me sneeze.

Peter: What a pity! Well, you ________________ (vorziehen) sports then, ________________?

Sally: Yes, I really like ________________ (Tischtennis) and ________________ (Sport, don't write sports) is my favourite subject.

Peter: I ________________ (zustimmen). I also like ________________ (Latein), ________________ (Gesundheitslehre) and ________________ (Geschichte).

While Peter and Sally ________________ (to look) at the notice board, Peter suddenly ________________ (to shout): Wow, there's a ________________ (theater) group!"

Sarah: Yes, and I ________________ (to be) in it soon, too! We have the best activities at our school, ________________ (nicht wahr)?

Peter: I ________________ (to write) an article for our school magazine next week. May I write an article about you?

Sally: OK but you don't want to write a _______________ (gruselig) story about me, _______________ (nicht wahr)?

Peter: Of course not. _______________ (könnten) we meet on Monday?

Sally I don't know, I have to check my _______________ (Stundenplan) first.

Good luck !

Lösung: 1. Schulaufgabe aus dem Englischen

I. Grammar

1. Fill in the correct preposition

In the afternoon my dad is often away *on* business. He usually works *at* home, sometimes also *at* night or *at* weekends. But *in* September he was *on* holiday *at* the seaside. When he came home *on* September 30th, he saw a lot of children *in* the street *in* front of our house. They were queuing up *in* pairs. What on earth were they doing there?

____/6

2. Simple past or Past progressive?

Simon and Robert *were playing* (play) football while Becky and Sarah *were watching* (watch) them. The two boys *were still playing* (still, play) when it *started* (start) to rain. So they all *went* (go) home. When Robert *arrived* (arrive), his Mum *was waiting* (wait) for him. Mrs. Croft: "Hi Robert! Can you imagine? I *fell* (fall) off my bike and *broke* (break) my arm!" Robert: "Oh, I´m really sorry, Mum!"

____/9

Tipps und Hinweise
Hier geht es um die Zeiten, hauptsächlich um die zwei Formen der ***Past tense***.
Zur Wiederholung: Alles was eindeutig vorbei ist, braucht eine ***Past tense***. Wenn eine Handlung geschah, während die andere schon im Gange war, nimmt man für die längere Handlung ***Past progressive*** *(was / were .... -ing)* und für die kürzere Handlung ***Simple past*** (***-ed*** oder zweite Verbform bei unregelmäßigen Verben).
Aber pass auf den Zusammenhang auf, denn nicht alle Sätze unten beschreiben etwas, was eindeutig vorbei ist!

3. Make comparisons

1. Ben Nevis is the *highest* (high) mountain. Mount Everest is *higher* (high) than Ben Nevis.
2. For me Harry Potter is one of *the most interesting* (interesting) books in the world. My sister thinks comics are *funnier than* (funny) books.
3. This English test was *the most difficult* (difficult) of all. No, I think it was *easier than* (easy) the last. A Math test is *worse than* (bad) a terrible cold. But one week in bed is *the worst* (bad) of all.
4. In Robin Hood's time the King was a *cruel* (cruel) man. Some of his sheriffs were *crueller than* (cruel)him. The Sheriff of Nottingham was *the cuellest* (cruel) of them all.

5. New York is a modern city. Munich is *not as big as* (big) New York, but it is *bigger than* (big) Augsburg.

6. Sailing is *more dangerous than* (dangerous) jogging, rock climbing is *the most dangerous* (dangerous) sport of the three.

____/15

Tipps und Hinweise
Wenn du vergleichst, sind zwei Sachen entweder gleich *(as ... as)* oder eine Sache ist größer/schneller, usw. *(bigger / faster than)*. Wenn drei oder mehr Dinge miteinander verglichen werden, kann eins davon das größte/schnellste, usw. sein *(the biggest / fastest)*. Wenn das Adjektiv zwei oder mehr Silben hat, heißt es bei der Steigerung z.B. *more important than* und bei der Höchststufe z.B. *the most important*. Ausnahmen sind *good / better / best* und *bad / worse / worst*.

4. Complete the sentences with question tags

a) You're interested in football, *aren't you*?

b) Dave has got a car, *hasn't he* ?

c) John wasn't in the theatre last year, *was he*?

d) They didn't show "Cats", *did they*?

e) Scott and Dave weren't there yesterday, *were they*?

____/5

Tipps und Hinweise
Bei den ***Question tags*** wird immer das Hilfsverb vom vorhergehenden Satz wiederholt. Ist kein Hilfsverb im Satz, nimmt man *do / does* oder *did*. Bei bejahten verneint man das ***Question tag***; ist der Satz verneint, dann muss das ***Question tag*** bejaht werden.

5. Ask for the underlined words

a) Sabrina <u>was telling a joke</u> when the teacher came in.

What was Sabrina doing when the teacher came in?

b) The boy grabbed <u>her bag.</u>

What did the boy grab?

c) Robin Hood protected the <u>poor peasants</u>.

Who did Robin Hood protect?

d) The peasants liked <u>Robin Hood</u> very much.

Who did the peasants like very much?

e) The man was talking to <u>the vistitors.</u>

Who was the man talking to?

f) He arrived at home <u>at nine o'clock.</u>

When did he arrive at home?

____/12

Tipps und Hinweise
Bei Fragen nimmt man ***who*** für Personen und ***what*** für Dinge. Andere Fragewörter sind ***when***, ***why*** oder ***how***.

II. Translation

1. Nächste Woche spiele ich auf der Bühne in der Schulhalle (Theater).

Next week I am going to act on the stage in the school hall.

2. Sandra gewann das Tennisspiel, nicht wahr?

Sandra won the tennis match, didn't she?

3. Während die Schüler einen Test schrieben, war ihre Lehrerin verschwunden.

While the pupils were writing a test, their teacher was gone.

4. Als die Lehrerin in das Klassenzimmer zurück rannte, ließ sie (plötzlich) ihre Schultasche fallen.

When the teacher ran back into the room she dropped her school bag.

5. Ein Schüler hinter ihr sah die Schultasche zu spät und stolperte über sie.

A pupil behind her saw the school bag too late and tripped over it. ____/15

III. Dialogue

Fill in the gaps. Be careful with the verb forms. Sometimes you need to fill in more than one word

One day in her lunch break, Sally *was reading* (to read) the notices at the activity board when she *heard* (to hear) a voice behind her. She *turned* (to turn) round and *saw* (to see) a boy.

Peter: Hi, I'm Peter. You're the new girl from Scotland, *aren't you?* What's your name?

Sally: Hello, nice to meet you. Do you like the activities at our school?

Peter: I'*m going to join* (beitreten) the pet club. I like animals. What about you?

Sally: I'm sorry. I can't because I'm *allergic to* (allergisch gegen) cats. They *make* me sneeze.

Peter: What a pity! Well, you *prefer* (vorziehen) sports then, *don't you?*

Sally: Yes, I really like *table tennis* (Tischtennis) and *PE* (Sport, don't write sports) is my favourite subject.

Peter: I *agree with you* (zustimmen). I also like *Latin* (Latein), *health* (Gesundheitslehre) and *history* (Geschichte).

While Peter and Sally *were looking* (to look) at the notice board, Peter suddenly *shouted* (to shout): Wow, there's a *drama* (theater) group!"

Sarah: Yes, and I *am going to be* (to be) in it soon, too! We have the best activities at our school, *haven't we* (nicht wahr)?

Peter: I*'m going to write* (to write) an article for our school magazine next week. May I write an article about you?

Sally: OK but you don't want to write a *scary* (gruselig) story about me, *do you* (nicht wahr)?

Peter: Of course not. *Could* (könnten) we meet on Monday?

Sally I don't know, I have to check my *timetable* (Stundenplan) first.

____/23

Total ____/85

1. Schulaufgabe aus dem Englischen

Name: ______________________________

Stoff: Unit 1–2, Focus 1

I. Vocabulary

1. Give *definitions* – use a *relative clause* or *contact clause* if possible

bully: ____

____

trap: ____

____

drama group: ____

____

2. Find *another verb* for the underlined words

I <u>like</u> English <u>better</u> than Latin. I really ____________________ English to Latin.

<u>Go on with</u> your fight for better grades. ____________________ fighting for them.

That's what my teacher <u>says again</u> and <u>again.</u> That's what my teacher always

________________.

3. Fill in the correct *preposition*

_______ March my dad was away _______ business _______ a nice town ______ the seaside. He and his partners _____________ all over the world always met _______ lunchtime or _____ the late afternoon. There were only three houses ___________ the street where his hotel was, and his hotel was _____________ a small bookshop and the old lighthouse.

II. Grammar

1. Fill in the correct *question tags* and the missing forms of *"to do"*

Tina: You know who our new English teacher is, ______________________?

Bob: Oh yes, of course I _________________ - everybody _______________! Why?

Tina: I only met him yesterday. He's not very friendly, ____________________?

Bob: Well, I think he's OK. I talked to him quite often. He's got a funny accent,

________________?

Tina: That's true. And I really ______________ like his long hair, it's terrible. But I'm a silly old girl, _______________?

Bob: Oh no, not at all! He _______________ look very attractive, that's right. But he helped the other new teachers to find their way, _____________________? ________________ you see him? I thought you were at school on that day, too!

2. Fill in the correct *verb forms*

Yesterday Carina ______________________________ home from school ____________ (mit dem Fahrrad fahren) when Wayne suddenly ________________ (anhalten) her.

He ____________________ (schnappen) her saddle and _________________ (veranlassen) her ________________________ (herunterspringen) her bike.

What ____________________________ (machen) at the weekend?

I __________________________________ (würde gerne beitreten) your tennis club and

I __________________________________ (möchte, dass du mitkommst),

he ________________________ (schreien).

While Carina ________________________ (suchen) someone to help her, Wayne's friends ____________________ (jubeln).These silly boys cannot _________________ (sich vorstellen) how a student from Germany _________________________ (sich fühlen müssen) when she is alone in an English town.

3. Use the correct forms of the adjectives and write *comparisons*

Sherwood Forest is one of the _________________________ (groß) forests in England. It is __________________________ (beliebt) than Nottingham Castle because England's ____________________________ (berühmt) outlaw lived there – Robin Hood. No other man was ______________________ (klug) than he was when hiding from the Sheriff, his __________________________ (schlimm) enemy. Robin's friends werde "merry" men, but Friar Tuck was ___________________ (lustig) of them all.

III. Mediation

Imagine you are Sarah, an English student who is in Bavaria at the moment. It's one day after Halloween, and you are writing an e-mail to Mary, your American cousin. Write this e-mail and use the following information. Don't forget to write a nice beginning (Mary wrote an e-mail to you last Sunday) and a good ending

Du erzählst von einer Einladung zu einer Halloween-Party im Jugendzentrum bei der Schule, zu der du mit einigen Jungs aus deiner Klasse gegangen bist. Dort trugen viele grausige Kostüme, aber niemand wusste eigentlich, wie dieser Brauch begann. Du fragst, warum die in Irland lebenden Kelten verkleidet in ihren Dörfern herumliefen und wie dann diese Tradition nach Amerika kam. Du erwähnst, dass es in England zwar auch Halloween-Parties gibt, aber dass die Kinder nicht von Tür zu Tür ziehen und um Geld bitten – das machen sie normalerweise fünf Tage später. Weiter berichtetest du, dass man auch in Deutschland vor vielen Häusern hohle Kürbisse sieht, die aber sicher kleiner sind als die amerikanischen Jack-O'Lanterns. – Du fragst deine Cousine, ob Halloween für sie einer der wichtigsten und aufregendsten Tage im Jahr ist. Außerdem willst du noch wissen, was sie an Weihnachten vorhat und ob sie dir die schönsten Fotos vom Tanz-Wettbewerb schicken könnte.

Good luck !

Lösung: 1. Schulaufgabe aus dem Englischen

I. Vocabulary

1. Give *definitions* – use a *relative clause* or *contact clause* if possible

bully: *A bully is a boy or a girl who is cruel to other children who are weaker.*

trap: *A trap is a thing you can catch mice with.*

drama group: *A drama group is subject in school for pupils who like playing theatre.*

____/10

2. Find *another verb* for the underlined words

I like English better than Latin. I really *prefer* English to Latin.

Go on with your fight for better grades. *Don't stop (Continue)* fighting for them.

That's what my teacher says again and again. That's what my teacher always *repeats / keeps saying.*

____/3

II. Grammar

1. Fill in the correct *question tags* and the missing forms of *"to do"*

Tina: You know who our new English teacher is, *don't you*?

Bob: Oh yes, of course I *do* – everybody *does*! Why?

Tina: I only met him yesterday. He's not very friendly, *is he*?

Bob: Well, I think he's OK. I talked to him quite often. He's got a funny accent, *hasn't he*?

Tina: That's true. And I really *don't* like his long hair, it's terrible. But I'm a silly old girl, *aren't I* ?

Bob: Oh no, not at all! He *doesn't* look very attractive, that's right. But he helped the other new teachers to find their way, *didn't he*? *Didn't* you see him? I thought you were at school on that day, too!

____/10

2. Fill in the correct *verb forms*

Yesterday Carina *was riding* home from school *by bike / oder: was cycling* home from school (mit dem Fahrrad fahren) when Wayne suddenly *stopped* (anhalten) her.

He *grabbed* (schnappen) her saddle and *made* (veranlassen) her *jump off* (herunterspringen) her bike.

What *are you going to do* (machen) at the weekend? I *would like to join* (würde gerne beitreten) your tennis club and I *want you to come with / I would like you to come along with me* (möchte, dass du mitkommst), he *shouted* (schreien).

While Carina *was looking for* (suchen) someone to help her, Wayne's friends *were cheering* (jubeln). These silly boys cannot *imagine* (sich vorstellen) how a student from Germany *must feel* (sich fühlen müssen) when she is alone in an English town. ____/16

3. Use the correct forms of the adjectives and write *comparisons*

Sherwood Forest is one of the *biggest* (groß) forests in England. It is *more popular* (beliebt) than Nottingham Castle because England's *most famous* (berühmt) outlaw lived there – Robin Hood. No other man was *cleverer* (klug) than he was when hiding from the Sheriff, his *worst* (schlimm) enemy. Robin's friends werde "merry" men, but Friar Tuck was *the funniest* (lustig) of them all.

____/6

Tipps und Hinweise
Wenn du vergleichst, sind zwei Sachen entweder gleich *(as ... as)* oder eine Sache ist größer/schneller, usw. *(bigger / faster than)*. Wenn drei oder mehr Dinge miteinander verglichen werden, kann eins davon das größte/schnellste, usw. sein *(the biggest / fastest)*. Wenn das Adjektiv zwei oder mehr Silben hat, heißt es bei der Steigerung z.B. *more important than* und bei der Höchststufe z.B. *the most important*. Ausnahmen sind *good / better / best* und *bad / worse / worst*.

4. Fill in the correct *preposition*

In March my dad was away *on* business *in* a nice town *at / on* the seaside. He and his partners *from* all over the world always met *at* lunchtime or *in* the late afternoon. There were only three houses *in* the street where his hotel was, and his hotel was *opposite* a small bookshop and the old lighthouse.

____/9

III. Mediation

Imagine you are Sarah, an English student who is in Bavaria at the moment. It's one day after Halloween, and you are writing an e-mail to Mary, your American cousin. Write this e-mail and use the following information. Don't forget to write a nice beginning (Mary wrote an e-mail to you last Sunday) and a good ending

Du erzählst von einer Einladung zu einer Halloween-Party im Jugendzentrum bei der Schule, zu der du mit einigen Jungs aus deiner Klasse gegangen bist. Dort trugen viele grausige Kostüme, aber niemand wusste eigentlich, wie dieser Brauch begann. Du fragst, warum die in Irland lebenden Kelten verkleidet in ihren Dörfern herumliefen und wie dann diese Tradition nach

Amerika kam. Du erwähnst, dass es in England zwar auch Halloween-Parties gibt, aber dass die Kinder nicht von Tür zu Tür ziehen und um Geld bitten – das machen sie normalerweise fünf Tage später. Weiter berichtetest du, dass man auch in Deutschland vor vielen Häusern hohle Kürbisse sieht, die aber sicher kleiner sind als die amerikanischen Jack-O'Lanterns. – Du fragst deine Cousine, ob Halloween für sie einer der wichtigsten und aufregendsten Tage im Jahr ist. Außerdem willst du noch wissen, was sie an Weihnachten vorhat und ob sie dir die schönsten Fotos vom Tanz-Wettbewerb schicken könnte.

Dear Mary,
How are you? I'm fine. Thanks for your last letter. It's great here in Germany. Can you imagine? I got an invitation to a Halloween party in the activity centre near my school where I went with some nice boys from my class. The people were wearing many scary costumes but actually nobody knew how this custom started. Why did the Irish Celts walk around in disguise in the villages? And how did this tradition get to America?
There are Halloween parties in England, too, but the children don't go from house to house. They do that 5 days later. You can see hollow pumpkins in Germany, too, but they're much smaller than the American Jack-O'Lanterns. Don't you think that Halloween is one of the most exciting days in the year? What do you want to do at Christmas? Could you also send me the most beautiful photos of the dancing competition, please?
Please write back soon,
Love,
Sarah

Alternative:
Dear Mary,
Thank you for your last letter.
Yesterday I was invited to a Halloween party in the activity centre near the school, and I went there with some boys from my class. Many people were wearing scary costumes, but nobody actually knew how this custom began. Why did the Celts in Ireland run around their villages in disguise? And how did this tradition later reach America? We also have Halloween parties in England, but (the) children don't go from door to door asking for money – they normally go five days later. In Germany you can see hollow pumpkins in front of a lot of houses, but they are really much smaller than (the) American Jack-O'Lanterns.
Is Halloween one of the most important and exciting days in the year for you, too?
Have you got any plans for Christmas this year?
And please, don't forget to send me the nicest photos from the dancing competition!
I look forward to your next letter.
Love,
Sarah

____/24

Total ____/78

2. Schulaufgabe aus dem Englischen

Name: ______________________________

Stoff: Unit 2–3A

I. Words

Give definitions! Use a relative clause or a contact clause if possible

1. bull's eye ____

____

2. brochure ____

____

3. stage ____

____

4. outlaw ____

____

II. Grammar

1. Fill in the correct future forms

F.C.Bayern's big match next Saturday ______________________ (stattfinden) in Berlin.

I'm sure F.C. Bayern______________________________ (haben) a real chance.

Dad and I ______________________________ (abfahren) for Berlin after lunch.

We ______________________________ (nehmen) some sandwiches and drinks with us.

Dad hopes that our fans ______________________________ (nicht machen) any trouble.

"I can't find my fan shirt, Mum!" – Don't worry, I ______________________ (helfen) you to look for it. It must be in your wardrobe.

2. Becky's class is doing a project about life in the Middle Ages. What does Becky tell her mother about the project? Use contact clauses. ***Questions for the history project***

What food did poor families eat?

What work did women do?

What games did children play?

What clothes did people wear?

What songs did people sing?

We're collecting information about ____________________

____

We 're finding out about ____________________

____

We're drawing pictures ____________________

____

We're listening to ____________________

____

We're writing about ____________________

____

3. Make one sentence out of two by using a relative clause
Use a contact clause where possible.* Begin *your sentence with the* underlined *word

1. <u>Robert</u> sits next to a boy at school. The name of the boy is Boris.

____

____

2. Robert plays with a boy. <u>The boy</u> is called Tim.

____

____

3. <u>Robert's teacher</u> showed a film about Robin Hood. Robin Hood helped the poor people.

____

____

4. <u>Robert</u> has got a cat. Her name is Tabby.

____

____

5. <u>Sarah</u> lives opposite Robert's house. She really is very nice.

____

____

6. Robert's father works for a computer company. <u>The company</u> is very famous.

____

____

7. There are a lot of machines at the computer company. They are very expensive.

____

____

8. Mrs Green is Robert's favourite teacher. She teaches German.

The____

____

III. Translation

In English, please. Use contact clauses when possible

1. Hat nicht Maid Marian die schönsten Haare?

____

____

2. Sie ist Robins Freundin, die ihm in dem gefährlichen Wettkampf hilft.

____

____

3. Little John ist ein Mann, den du auch um Hilfe bitten kannst.

____

____

4. Die Menge jubelte, als die Wettkämpfer, die ihre langen Bogen trugen, zur Tribüne gingen.

____

____

5. Unter der großen Eiche, ein Baum, in dem du dich verstecken kannst, hatten Robin und seine Männer das lustigste Abendessen.

____

____

IV. Text Production

Write a letter of eight sentences to Annie Logan and tell her what you like and dislike about Radio Nottingham

Dear Annie Logan,

Good luck !

Lösung: 2. Schulaufgabe aus dem Englischen

I. Words

Give definitions! Use a relative clause or a contact clause if possible

1. bull's eye *The bull's eye is the place which is in the middle of the target.*
2. brochure *A brochure is a thing you read when you want some information about a new product.*
3. stage *The stage is the place where you see the people who act in a play.*
4. outlaw *An outlaw is somebody who fights against the Sheriff.*

____/8

II. Grammar

1. Fill in the correct future forms

F.C. Bayern's big match next Saturday *will be* (stattfinden) in Berlin. I'm sure F.C. Bayern *will have* (haben) a real chance. Dad and I *are going to leave* (abfahren) for Berlin after lunch. We *are going to take* (nehmen) some sandwiches and drinks with us. Dad hopes that our fans *won't make* (nicht machen) any trouble. "I can't find my fan shirt, Mum!" – Don't worry, I*'ll help* (helfen) you look for it. It must be in your wardrobe.

____/6

Tipps und Hinweise
Hier sollst du dich zwischen der ***will future*** und der ***going to future*** entscheiden.
Will nimmt man bei spontanen Entschlüssen und nach den Verben *I think, I feel, I hope, I'm sure.*
"Am / are / is going to ...." nimmt man, wenn der Entschluss schon feststeht.

2. Becky's class is doing a project about life in the Middle Ages. What does Becky tell her mother about the project? Use contact clauses. *Questions for the history project.*

What food did poor families eat?

What work did women do?

What games did children play?

What clothes did people wear?

What songs did people sing?

We're collecting information about *the food poor families ate.*

We 're finding out about *the work woman did.*

We're drawing pictures of *the games children played.*

We're writing about *clothes people wore.*

We're listening to *songs people sang in the Middle Ages.*

____/12

3. Make one sentence out of two by using a relative clause

Use a contact clause where possible.* Begin *your sentence with the* underlined *word

1. Robert sits next to a boy at school. The name of the boy is Boris.

Robert sits next to a boy at school whose name is Boris.

2. Robert often plays with a boy. The boy is called Tim.

The boy Robert often plays with is called Tim.

3. Robert's teacher showed a film about Robin Hood. Robin Hood helped the poor people.

Robert's teacher showed a film about Robin Hood, who helped the poor people.

4. Robert has got a cat. Her name is Tabby.

Robert has got a cat whose name is Tabby.

5. Sarah lives opposite Robert's house. She really is very nice.

Sarah, who really is very nice, lives opposite Robert's house.

6. Robert's father works for a computer company. The company is very famous.

The company Robert's father works for is very famous.

7. There are a lot of machines at the computer company. They are very expensive.

There are a lot of machines in the computer company which are very expensive.

8. Mrs Green is Robert's favourite teacher. She teaches German.

The teacher who teaches German is Robert's favourite teacher Mrs Green.

____/16

III. Translation

In English, please. Use contact clauses when possible

1. Hat nicht Maid Marian die schönsten Haare?

Hasn't Maid Marian got the most beautiful hair?

Maid Marian has got the most beautiful hair, doesn't she?

2. Sie ist Robins Freundin, die ihm in dem gefährlichen Wettkampf hilft.

She is Robin's girlfriend who helps him in the dangerous competition.

3. Little John ist ein Mann, den du auch um Hilfe bitten kannst.

Little John is the man you can ask for help, too.

4. Die Menge jubelte, als die Wettkämpfer, die ihre langen Bogen trugen, zur Tribüne gingen.

The crowd cheered when the competitors who carried their long bows were going to the platform / stage.

5. Unter der großen Eiche, ein Baum, in dem du dich verstecken kannst, hatten Robin und seine Männer das lustigste Abendessen.

Under the big oak, a tree (in which) you can hide in Robin and his men had the funniest dinner.

____/15

IV. Text Production

Write a letter of eight sentences to Annie Logan and tell her what you like and dislike about Radio Nottingham

Dear Annie Logan,

I like Radio Nottingham's breakfast show.

I like that you gave other people the chance to win two tickets for the rock concert.

I dislike that you don't open me the chance to win a ticket for the football match.

I like the songs you are playing.

I don't like the telephone quiz.

I like that you give information about the weather, news and events.

I don't like your question.

I like that you give some information about the news.

Yours sincerely ...

____/16

Total ____/73

2. Schulaufgabe aus dem Englischen

Name: ______________________________

Stoff: Focus 1, Unit 2

I. Words

Give definitions! Explain the following words. Use relative clauses

a) Sir Guy of Gisborne

____

b) Halloween

____

c) Alan a Dale

____

d) a castle

____

e) the Normans

____

II. Grammar

Sentences with comparisons

Fill in the correct form of the adjective (++ superlative; + comparative, = the same).

Bud, a boy from Texas, is visiting David in Nottingham. They go to the Sherwood Forest Visitor Centre together with David's friend Paul. Bud thinks that everything is better in Texas

Paul: "Where in Texas are you from, Bud?

Bud: "I'm from Dallas, the ________________________ (beautiful; ++) city in the USA. It also has the ________________________ (busy; ++) airport in the world."

Paul: "That's the ______________________ (silly; ++) thing I've ever heard! New York has _____________________ (good; +) and also ____________________ (high; +) skyscrapers than Dallas. And Dallas is ____________________ (small; +) than New York."

Bud: "I'm sure people aren't ________________________________(friendly; +) and _____________________ (funny; +) in New York than people in Texas! New Yorkers also drive a lot ________________________ (bad; +) than Texans!"

Paul: "Oh, come on! For you cars are___________________________ (important; ++)

thing in the word, I can't understand that. I think cars are the __________________ (boring; ++) thing in the world."

David: "You like planes. I think cars are just ________ __________________ (interesting; =) planes. But stop arguing now – let's watch that film about Robin Hood, England's __________________ (famous; ++) folk hero. Today, he still is __________________ (popular; +) than anybody else here in England."

Bud: "OK, and let's have lunch after that – I'm sure I'm __________________ (hungry; +) than you are; I need a sandwich!"

III. Translation

1. Niemand wusste, dass Marian den Geächteten oftmals Informationen über den Sheriff zukommen ließ.

____

____

2. Robin fühlte sich sicher, weil er verkleidet war und aussah wie ein armer Kleinbauer.

____

____

3. Viele der Wettkampfteilnehmer befanden sich schon auf dem großen Platz vor dem Schloss.

____

____

IV. Ask for underlined words

1. The children were playing football <u>in the garden</u>.

____

2. Robert did his English homework <u>in the afternoon.</u>

____

3. Sarah is listening to her <u>favourite band.</u>

____

4. Dave always looks after his <u>neighbours dog.</u>

____

5. <u>Rock climbing</u> is more dangerous than jogging.

____ **Good luck !**

Lösung: 2. Schulaufgabe aus dem Englischen

I. Words

Give definitions! Explain the following words. Use relative clauses

a) Sir Guy of Gisborne

Sir Guy of Gisborne was a man who told the Sheriff bad news.

Alternative: Sir Guy of Gisborne was a man who lived in the Middle Ages.

b) Halloween

Halloween is the day which comes before All Saints' Day.

Alternative: Halloween is a day for people who like to dress up as ghosts.

c) Alan a Dale

Alan a Dale was a man who made music for Robin Hood.

Alternative: Alan a Dale was a singer who lived in Nottingham in the Middle Ages.

d) a castle

A castle is a huge grey building which is sometimes very old.

Alternative: A castle is a very big stone house which was built for a nobleman many years ago.

e) the Normans

The Normans who came from France conquered the Saxons in the late 1100s.

Alternative: The Normans were the people whose king was William the Conqueror.

____/10

II. Grammar

Sentences with comparisons

Fill in the correct form of the adjective (++ superlative; + comparative, = the same).

Bud, a boy from Texas, is visiting David in Nottingham. They go to the Sherwood Forest Visitor Centre together with David's friend Paul. Bud thinks that everything is better in Texas

Paul: "Where in Texas are you from, Bud?

Bud: "I'm from Dallas, the *most beautiful* (beautiful; ++) city in the USA. It also has the *busiest* (busy; ++) airport in the world."

Paul: "That's the *silliest* (silly; ++) thing I've ever heard! New York has *better* (good; +) and also *higher* (high; +) skyscrapers than Dallas. And Dallas is *smaller* (small; +) than New York."

Bud: "I'm sure people aren't *friendlier* (friendly; +) and *funnier* (funny; +) in New York than people in Texas.! New Yorkers also drive a lot *worse* (bad; +) than Texans!"

Paul: "Oh, come on! For you cars are *the most important* (important; ++) thing in the word, I can't understand that. I think cars are the *most boring* (boring; ++) thing in the world."

David: "You like planes. I think cars are just *as interesting as* (interesting; =) planes. But stop arguing now – let's watch that film about Robin Hood, England's *most famous* (famous; ++) folk hero. Today, he still is *more popular* (popular; +) than anybody else here in England."

Bud: "OK, and let's have lunch after that – I'm sure I'm *hungrier* (hungry; +) than you are; I need a sandwich!" ____/15

Tipps und Hinweise
Wenn du vergleichst, sind zwei Sachen entweder gleich *(as ... as)* oder eine Sache ist größer/schneller, usw. *(bigger / faster than)*. Wenn drei oder mehr Dinge miteinander verglichen werden, kann eins davon das größte/schnellste, usw. sein *(the biggest / fastest)*. Wenn das Adjektiv zwei oder mehr Silben hat, heißt es bei der Steigerung z.B. *more important than* und bei der Höchststufe z.B. *the most important*. Ausnahmen sind *good / better / best* und *bad / worse / worst*.

III. Translation

1. Niemand wusste, dass Marian den Geächteten oftmals Informationen über den Sheriff zukommen ließ.

Nobody knew that Marian often gave the outlaws information about the Sheriff.

Alternative: Nobody knew that Marian often told the outlaws important things about the Sheriff.

2. Robin fühlte sich sicher, weil er verkleidet war und aussah wie ein armer Kleinbauer.

Robin felt safe because he was in disguise and looked like a poor peasant.

Alternative: Robin felt safe because he was disguised as a poor peasant.

3. Viele der Wettkampfteilnehmer befanden sich schon auf dem großen Platz vor dem Schloss.

Many of the competitors were already in the big court in front of the castle.

Alternative: Many competitors were already gathering in the big area in front of the castle.

____/15

IV. Ask for underlined words

1. The children were playing football in the garden. *Where were the children playing football?*
2. Robert did his English homework in the afternoon. *When did Robert do his English homework?*
3. Sarah is listening to her favourite band. *What is Sarah listening to?*
4. Dave always looks after his neighbours' dog. *What does Dave always look after?*
5. Rock climbing is more dangerous than jogging. *What is more dangerous than jogging?* ____/15

Total ____/55

3. Schulaufgabe aus dem Englischen

Name: ______________________________

Stoff: Unit 3–5

I. Vocabulary

a. Find the words

1. mountain (Gegenteil) ____________________

2. This is how you feel when you hope something will happen and it doesn't: ______________

3. If you aren't joking but really mean what you are saying you are _______________________

4. word – sentence – ______________________

5. Name two popular water sports for which you need a boat.

____________________ ______________________

6. ______________ – summer ________________ – winter.

7. A _______________________ plan is a plan you aren't going to change.

8. almost = ____________________

b. Definitions: Write at least one complete sentence for each word

1. rescue ____

____

2. strawberry ____

____

II. Grammar

a. Talking about the future: will or going to

1.What __________________________ (you do) in the summer holidays?

I _______________________ (stay) in the Lake District. Oh really? I'm sure you

___________________________________ (have a good time). – Yes, I hope I

__________________.

2. Friday is the 13th. I think something terrible __________________ (happen). Don't be so

silly! I know what, I _________________________ (make) you a cup of tea. Then you

_____________________ (feel) better.

b. Complete !

Infinitive	**Past tense**	**Past participle**
to meet		
to read		
to hear		
to hide		
to win		
to catch		

c. A letter from the Lake District: Past tense or Present perfect?

Becky and Simon are spending a week in the Lake District. This is Becky's letter to Sarah

Dear Sarah,

This week ____________________ (be) quite exciting so far. We __________________ ________________ (just come back) from a trip to Ullswater. But more about that later. When we arrived at the hotel on Monday it was closed. But we ________________ (find) a nice bed and breakfast place. The owners are called Mr and Mrs Preston.

__________________ you __________________ (ever stay) at a bed and breakfast?

I ______________________(never see) this part of Britain. But my parents ____________________ (live) near Derwentwater years ago.

My Dad once ___________________________ (tell) me some ghost stories of Old Moses.

The Prestons are nice people. They _____________________(show) us a lot of interesting things so far. Yesterday we ____________________(speak) to Tom, the Milkman, about the activities you can do here. He________________________ (give) me a book about smugglers.

I must stop now, Sarah. Simon is screaming in the kitchen downstairs. I hope he ____________________ (not cut) his finger!

Yours Becky

III. Mediation

You are visiting your grandparents and you are talking about last week, which you spent in Keswick

Dein Opa möchte wissen, ob du auf dem Derwentwater zum Rudern gegangen bist.

Grandpa: ____

Du bejahst und fragst ihn, ob er jemals schon im Lake District war.

You: ____

____

Dein Opa verneint, aber er fügt hinzu, dass er schon eine Menge über diese schöne Landschaft gehört hat.

____

____

Deine Oma steckt den Kopf zur Tür herein und fragt, ob du schon Mittag gegessen hast. Sie bietet dir Hühnchen mit Reis an.

Grandma: ____

____

Du lehnst dankend ab und erklärst, dass du dich erst vor eine Stunde mit Tante Lucy in Angelos Restaurant getroffen hast.

You: ____

____

Du schilderst deinen Großeltern, was du gegesessen hast. Vorspeise: Tomatensuppe. Hauptspeise: Fisch mit Kartoffeln. Nachspeise: Obstsalat.

You: ____

____

Du willst wissen, ob deine Großeltern schon mal Angelos Obstsalat probiert haben. Der ist köstlich.

You: ____

____

IV. Text Production: A phone call

You surely remember the story of Jenny's adventure on Great Gable.

Imagine you are Mr Preston. It's 5 p.m. and the Leinerts are still out on Great Gable.

Mr Preston is worried, so he phones the Mountain Rescue people.

Write about 80 words and use the following words in your phone call:

slippery / weather forecast / warn / accident / set off / careful / fog

MR: Derentwater 670224

Mr Preston: Hello, this is Mr Preston speaking.

MR: Hello Mr Preston, what can we do for you?

Mr Preston:.

Good luck !

Lösung: 3. Schulaufgabe aus dem Englischen

I. Vocabulary

a. Find the words

1. mountain (Gegenteil): *valley*

2. This is how you feel when you hope something will happen and it doesn't: *disappointed*

3. If you aren't joking but really mean what you are saying you are *serious.*

4. word – sentence – *text*

5. Name two popular water sports for which you need a boat.

canoeing *kayaking* *(rowing)*

6. *spring* – summer – *autumn* – winter.

7. A *schedule* plan is a plan you aren't going to change.

8. almost = *nearly* ____/10

b. Definitions: Write at least one complete sentence for each word

1. rescue *Rescue is help you get when you are hurt.*

2. strawberry *It's a red little fruit which a lot of people love.*
You can also make jam with strawberries.

____/4

II. Grammar

a. Talking about the future: will or going to

1. What *are you going to do* (you do) in the summer holidays? I *am going to stay* (stay) in the Lake District. – Oh really? I'm sure you *will have a good time* (have a good time). – Yes, I hope I *will.*

2. Friday is the 13th. I think something terrible *will happen* (happen). Don't be so silly! I know what, I *will make* (make) you a cup of tea. Then you *will feel* (feel) better.

____/8

Tipps und Hinweise
Hier sollst du dich zwischen der ***will future*** und der ***going to future*** entscheiden.
Will nimmt man bei spontanen Entschlüssen und nach den Verben *I think, I feel, I hope, I'm sure.*
"*Am / are / is going to ...*" nimmt man, wenn der Entschluss schon feststeht.

b. Complete

Tipps und Hinweise
Hier sind 6 unregelmäßige Verben. Die drei Formen muss man einfach auswendig lernen!

Infinitive	**Past tense**	**Past participle**
meet	*met*	*met*
read	*read*	*read*
hear	*heard*	*heard*
hide	*hid*	*hidden*
win	*won*	*won*
catch	*caught*	*caught*

____/6

c. A letter from the Lake District: Past tense or Present perfect?

Becky and Simon are spending a week in the Lake District. This is Becky's letter to Sarah

Dear Sarah,

this week *has been* (be) quite exciting so far. We *'ve just come back* (just come back) from a trip to Ullswater. But more about that later. When we arrived at the hotel on Monday it was closed. But we *found* (find) a nice bed and breakfast place. The owners are called Mr and Mrs Preston. *Have* you *ever stayed* (ever stay) at a bed and breakfast?

I *have never seen* (never see) this part of Britain. But my parents *lived* (live) near Derwentwater years ago.

My Dad once *told* (tell) me some ghost stories of Old Moses.

The Prestons are nice people. They *have shown* (show) us a lot of interesting things so far.

Yesterday we *spoke* (speak) to Tom, the milkman, about the activities you can do here. He *gave* (give) me a book about smugglers.

I must stop now, Sarah. Simon is screaming in the kitchen downstairs. I hope he *hasn't cut* (not cut) his finger!

____/11

Yours,

Becky

Tipps und Hinweise
Denke daran, wenn etwas eindeutig vorbei ist, brauchst du ***Past tense*** (entweder ***Simple past*** oder ***Past progressive***). Wenn etwas gerade passiert ist (ohne genaue Zeitangabe), oder schon mal passiert ist (auch ohne Zeitangabe), oder noch nie passiert ist, nimmst du das ***Present perfect***.

III. Mediation

You are visiting your grandparents and you are talking about last week, which you spent in Keswick

Dein Opa möchte wissen, ob du auf dem Derwentwater zum Rudern gegangen bist.

Grandpa: Did you row on the Derwentwater?

Alternative: Did you do any rowing on the Derwentwater?

Du bejahst und fragst ihn, ob er jemals schon im Lake District war.

You: Yes, I did. Have you ever been to the Lake District?

Dein Opa verneint, aber er fügt hinzu, dass er schon eine Menge über diese schöne Landschaft gehört hat.

No, I haven't. But I've already heard a lot about this beautiful landscape.

Deine Oma steckt den Kopf zur Tür herein und fragt, ob du schon Mittag gegessen hast. Sie bietet dir Hühnchen mit Reis an.

Grandma: Have you had lunch yet? Do you want to have chicken with rice?

Alternative: Would you like some chicken with rice?

Du lehnst dankend ab und erklärst, dass du dich erst vor einer halben Stunde mit Tante Lucy in Angelos Restaurant getroffen hast.

You: No, thank you. I only just met Aunt Lucy in Angelo's Restaurant half an hour ago.

Du schilderst deinen Großeltern, was du gegessen hast. Vorspeise: Tomatensuppe. Hauptspeise: Fisch mit Kartoffeln. Nachspeise: Obstsalat.

You: I had tomato soup as a starter; fish with potatoes as a main course and fruit salad as a dessert.

Du willst wissen, ob deine Großeltern schon mal Angelos Obstsalat probiert haben. Der ist köstlich.

You: Have you ever tried / tasted Angelo's fruit salad? It's delicious.

____/18

IV. Text Production: A phone call

You surely remember the story of Jenny's adventure on Great Gable.

Imagine you are Mr Preston. It's 5 p.m. and the Leinerts are still out on Great Gable.

Mr Preston is worried, so he phones the Mountain Rescue people.

Write about 80 words and use the following words in your phone call:

slippery / weather forecast / warn / accident / set off / careful / fog

MR (Mountain Rescue): Derentwater 670224

MP (= Mr Preston): Hello, this is Mr Preston speaking.

MR: Hello Mr Preston, what can we do for you?

MP: I'm phoning you because our guests, the Leinerts, haven't come back from their tour. They ***set off*** *this morning to climb (up) Great Gable. The* ***weather forecast*** *for today was very good at 7 a.m. but I* ***warned*** *them not to go on if the weather changes. I told them that the paths can get* ***slippery*** *if it rains. Maybe they've had an* ***accident*** *because they haven't been* ***careful****.*

MR: Oh dear! Now it's very ***foggy*** *up on Great Gable. I think we'll send a team up there to look for them.*

MP: Great! It'sa family of four. I hope you'll find them. Thank you. Goodbye.

MR: We'll do our best. Goodbye.

Alternative:

MR (=Mountain Rescue): Derentwater 670224

MP (= Mr Preston): Hello, this is Mr Preston speaking.

MR: Hello Mr Preston, what can we do for you?

MP: I am worried about our guests, a family of four. Maybe they have had an ***accident****. They* ***set off*** *for Great Garble early this morning, when the* ***weather forecast*** *was still good. I* ***warned*** *them that the paths could get very slippery when there is rain or* ***fog****. Now it is 5 pm and they still haven't come back. Maybe they weren't* ***careful*** *enough when the weather changed.*

MR: Oh dear! We will send a team to look for them immediately.

MP: Thank you! Please phone me when you find them, okay?

MR: I will. Goodbye.

____/20

Total ____/77

3. Schulaufgabe aus dem Englischen

Name: ______________________________

Stoff: Unit 5–6

I. Dictation

II. Grammar

1. Complete the following sentences with the right tense and find the right verbs

Two weeks ago I _____________ my pony and _____________ my arm.

Dad _____________ to hospital by car.

There the doctor asked me: " _____________ (ever) to hospital before?"

"Yes," I answered, "I _____________ here last week with a broken leg."

"_____________ you _____________ breakfast yet? he asked.

"No_____________ . But I_____________ a big dinner last night."

2. Will or going to? Fill in

On Saturday Robert and I _______________________ see Manchester against Arsenal.

It is certain that Arsenal _______________________ play with its top players.

Dad _______________________ drive up to Manchester.

Of course I hope Manchester United _______________________ win.

Robert is sure they _______________________ (not beat) Arsenal.

I must go now. Mum _______________________ meet me in town at 5 o'clock.

III. Text Production

You are at an Indian restaurant and want to order a three-course-meal. At the end you pay.
Write a dialogue of six sentences

Waiter: ____

I: ____

Waiter: ____

I: ____

Waiter: ____

I: ____

Waiter: ____

I: ____

IV. Translation

1. War es nicht sonnig, als wir aus dem Auto stiegen?

2. Es war sogar warm!

3. Wir brauchten unsere Anoraks nicht.

4. Bist du jemals Great Gable hinaufgestiegen?

5. Es ist immer aufregend, weil du die Wolken, den Nebel und manchmal einen Mann mit einem schwarzen Hut siehst.

6. Hast du jemals junge Leute mit einem gebrochenen Fuß in den Bergen gefunden?

7. Ja! Dann hoffe ich, dass der Akku deines Handys nicht leer geworden ist.

Good luck !

Lösung: 3. Schulaufgabe aus dem Englischen

I. Dictation

The young people's wrong clothes. The weather forecast for Tuesday was actually quite good. But the people who live around Great Gable usually warn their guests: "Don't go if the weather changes and take warm sweat-shirts, extra anoraks and strong shoes". But Judy and Kevin, two teenagers from London, were just bored. "It's a beautiful day, there is not a cloud in the sky, why spend some extra money on new clothes?" Kevin said. So they set off, Judy with a T-shirt and jeans, Kevin with shorts and tennis shoes. It was especially sunny and warm when they started to climb. The path became steeper and steeper. After half an hour the first dark cloud appeared, and when the first one was over, it started to rain, it got cold and the path was slippery. "Kevin, I'm wet through and through." Judy cried." Let's turn back", Judy said. So they hurried down the path until Kevin fell. He grabbed Judy and tried to get up, but his left foot hurt. He staggered but could not stand. Judy saw how dangerous the situation was. She switched on her mobile and called the Moon – the Rescue people.

____/20

II. Grammar

1. Complete the following sentences with the right tense and find the right verbs

Two weeks ago I *was trekking on* my pony and *broke* my arm. Dad *drove me* to hospital by car.

There the doctor asked me: "*Have you ever been* (ever) to hospital before?"

"Yes," I answered, "I *was* here last week with a broken leg."

"*Have* you *had* breakfast yet? he asked.

"No, *I haven't.* But I *had* a big dinner last night."

____/8

2. Will or going to? Fill in

On Saturday Robert and I *are going to* see Manchester against Arsenal.

It is certain that Arsenal *will* play with its top players.

Dad *is going to* drive up to Manchester.

Of course I hope Manchester United *will* win.

Robert is sure they *won't beat* (not beat) Arsenal.

I must go now. Mum *is going to* meet me in town at 5 o'clock.

____/6

III. Text Production

You are at an Indian restaurant and want to order a three-course-meal. At the end you pay.
Write a dialogue of six sentences

Waiter: *Hello, are you ready to order now? What do you want to drink and eat?*

I: *Yes I am. As a starter I think I'll have a mixed salad. For the main course I want a steak.*

Waiter: *Do you prefer it with potatoes or with Indian rice?*

I: *I prefer it with Indian rice. Can I have a bottle of water and an orange juice, too?*

Waiter: *Do you want a dessert?*

I: *Yes, please. I'd like a fruit salad.*

Waiter: *OK, have a good dinner.*

I: *Oh yes, I'm sure I will.*

____/20

IV. Translation

1. War es nicht sonnig, als wir aus dem Auto stiegen?

Wasn't it sunny when we got out of the car?

2. Es war sogar warm!

Actually it was warm.

3. Wir brauchten unsere Anoraks nicht.

We didn't need our anoraks.

4. Bist du jemals Great Gable hinaufgestiegen?

Have you ever climbed Great Gable?

5. Es ist immer aufregend, weil du die Wolken, den Nebel und manchmal einen Mann mit einem schwarzen Hut siehst.

It's always exciting because you see the clouds, the fog and sometimes a man with a black hat.

6. Hast du jemals junge Leute mit einem gebrochenen Fuß in den Bergen gefunden?

Have you ever found young people with a broken foot in the mountains?

7. Ja! Dann hoffe ich, dass der Akku deines Handys nicht leer geworden ist.

Yes, I have. Then I hope that the battery of your mobile hasn't run down.

____/20

Total ____/74

4. Schulaufgabe aus dem Englischen

Name: ____________________________

Stoff : Unit 6–7

I. Dictation

– see solution: write text on an extra sheet –

II. Grammar

1. Ask for the underlined words

I went to the school party last night.	______________________________
Tom gave me the new CD.	______________________________
George came at eight o'clock.	______________________________
We have known Tom since 1997.	______________________________
I have known David for eight years.	______________________________
He had to come home at six o'clock.	______________________________
We helped David to do his homework.	______________________________
David always helps John.	______________________________

2. Past tense and future tense

a) Put the sentences into the Past tense. Use the substitutes

Robert can't go to Nottingham.	______________________________
May you go to the festival.	______________________________
Eric needn't clean the kitchen.	______________________________

b) Put the sentences into the Future tense. Use the substitutes

Can you play the piano?	______________________________
Kevin may not drink alcohol.	______________________________
Alan must close the windows.	______________________________

3. Put in the missing forms to express ability, permission or obligation. Be careful: Sometimes you must use the negative form

Sally Gooch and her friends were lucky. Although they __________________ give their cookies to the children at the hospital, they ____________________ help them in the end. But they ______________________________ organize their project better next time!

________ the other students (apart from Bruce and Sven) ______________________ miss any classes? No, they weren't. They _____________ finish their projects on Saturday, so they ________________________ go on with them on Monday.

All the projects were a success, and the 8th graders hope they __________________ ______ help the community again in the future.

III. Translate

Susan und Dave unterhalten sich am ersten Schultag über ihre Ferien. Susan: "Bist du im Juli mit deinen Eltern nach Schottland gefahren?"

____

____

Dave: "Ja. Wir wollten eigentlich drei Wochen dort bleiben, aber nach drei Tagen fing es an zu regnen und es hörte acht Tage (lang) nicht auf. Also fuhren wir wieder nach Hause. Was hast du in den Ferien gemacht?"

____

____

____

Susan: „Wir hatten auch etwas anderes geplant, aber dann wurde mein Bruder krank und wir mussten zu Hause bleiben. Aber ich konnte es optimal ausnutzen, weil unsere netten Nachbarn sagten: „Wenn du auf unser Haus aufpasst, darfst du unser Schwimmbad jederzeit benutzen."

____

____

____

Good luck !

Lösung: 4. Schulaufgabe aus dem Englischen

I. Dictation

Make a Difference Day

Make a Difference Day is the largest national day for helping others – a celebration of neighbours helping neighbours. It takes place on the fourth Saturday of every October. It's quite an experience to watch people, young and old, when they carry out a project that is useful to others. Some raise money and give it to old people's homes or to a charity. Others collect clothes for poor families in their neighbourhood. Then there are people who go to the parks and pick up trash there. Very often it takes them a lot of time to organize their projects, but in the end they all believe that they have an obligation to help their community.

Kristi Lepage, who works for Denver's Earth Club, says: "It's a fact that in 2003, for example, about three million people all over the world did exceptional things to show their interest for those who do not live on the sunny side of life."

____/23

II. Grammar

1. Ask for the underlined words

I went to the school party last night.	*Where did you go to last night?*
Tom gave me the new CD.	*What did Tom give you?*
George came at eight o'clock.	*Who came at eight o'clock?*
We have known Tom since 1997.	*Who have you known since 1997?*
I have known David for eight years.	*How long have you known David?*
He had to come home at six o'clock.	*When did he have to come home?*
We helped David to do his homework.	*Who did we help to do his homework?*
David always helps John.	*Who does David always help?*

____/16

2. Past tense and Future tense

a) Put the sentences into the Past tense. Use the substitutes

Robert can't go to Nottingham.	*Robert wasn't able to go to Nottingham.*
May you go to the festival.	*Were you allowed to go to the festival?*
Eric needn't clean the kitchen.	*Eric didn't have to clean the kitchen.*

b) Put the sentences into the Future tense. Use the substitutes

Can you play the piano?	*Will you be able to play the piano?*
Kevin may not drink alcohol.	*Kevin won't be allowed to drink alcohol.*
Alan must close the windows.	*Alan will have to close the windows.*

____/12

Tipps und Hinweise
Pass genau auf, in welcher Zeit jeder einzelne Satz ist! Du must wählen zwischen ***Future tense*** (wenn etwas in Zukunft geschieht) oder ***Past tense*** (wenn etwas eindeutig vorbei ist). Wenn etwas gerade passiert ist (ohne genaue Zeitangabe), oder schon mal passiert ist (auch ohne Zeitangabe), oder noch nie passiert ist, nimmst du das ***Present perfect***.
Für die Hilfsverben ***must, can, may, mustn't*** brauchst du die Ersatzverben *to have to, to be able to* und *(not) to be allowed to.*

3. Put in the missing forms to express ability, permission or obligation. Be careful: Sometimes you must use the negative form

Sally Gooch and her friends were lucky. Although they *weren't allowed to* give their cookies to the children at the hospital, they *were able to* help them in the end. But they *will have to* organize their project better next time!

Were the other students (apart from Bruce and Sven) *allowed to* miss any classes? No, they weren't. They *had to* finish their projects on Saturday, so they *didn't have to* go on with them on Monday.

All the projects were a success, and the 8th graders hope they *will be able to* help the community again in the future.

III. Translate

Susan und Dave unterhalten sich am ersten Schultag über ihre Ferien. Susan: "Bist du im Juli mit deinen Eltern nach Schottland gefahren?"
Susan and Dave are talking about their holidays on the first day of school. Susan: "Did you go to Scotland with your parents in July?"
Dave: "Ja. Wir wollten eigentlich drei Wochen dort bleiben, aber nach drei Tagen fing es an zu regnen und es hörte acht Tage (lang) nicht auf. So fuhren wir wieder nach Hause. Was hast du in den Ferien gemacht?"

Dave: „Yes, we did. Actually we wanted to stay there for three weeks but after three days it started to rain and it didn't stop for eight days. So we went home again. What did you do in your holidays?"
Susan: „Wir hatten auch etwas anderes geplant, aber dann wurde mein Bruder krank und wir mussten zu Hause bleiben. Aber ich konnte es optimal ausnutzen, weil unsere netten Nachbarn sagten: „Wenn du auf unser Haus aufpasst, darfst du unser Schwimmbad jederzeit benutzen.""
"Susan: „We had also planned something different but then my brother became / got ill and we had to stay at home. But I could make the most of it because our nice (friendly) neighbours said: "If you look after our house you may use our swimming pool at any time.""

____/15

Total ____/76

4. Schulaufgabe aus dem Englischen

Name: ______________________________

Stoff: Unit 5–6

I. Vocabulary and grammar

1. Fill in suitable English words – sometimes the first letter is given, sometimes a German word is given. Be careful with the nouns (singular or plural?) and the verb forms (right tense). If there is a verb given with a P (for permission), an A (for ability) or an O (for obligation) behind it, it means that you must use this verb with the correct form of the auxiliary or its substitute

Cooper Middle School is in Denver, Colorado. It offers its 480 students a b___________ program of classes and a_______________. The mission of Cooper Middle School is to keep up its long tradition of giving a good education to students from all ______________ (Arten) of social backgrounds. The school's ____________ (Ziel) is to ______________ (vorbereiten) its students for s____________ in college and life. To do that, the students always ____________ (teilnehmen an) a very special day on the fourth Saturday in October.

So, what projects __________ the students __________ (machen) last year? Of course, the students ________________ (talk O) about their plans first. They had a lot of ideas. Tina for example wanted to pick up ____________ (Abfall) in the park. But Sally said: "If we pick up trash, we ________________ (brauchen) a lot of bags. And it will be boring!" Tina answered: "Typical! If it ____________________ (sich nach Arbeit anhören) Sally isn't interested."

But in the end they all found really good things to do.

José ________________ (not look O) far for his project. He and his father's band Corazón de Oro did some concerts and with the money they e______________ they _________________ (buy A) three small trees for the school. So the front of the school __________________ (aussehen) nice _________ (wenn) they have planted the trees. All the students ______________ ______________ (finish O) their projects on Saturday, only Bruce and Sven ______________________________ (verpassen P) two classes on Monday because they ___________________________________ (not go A) to the elementary schools on Saturday to deliver (= abgeben) their books. Sally and Tina made some cookies for the _________________________ (Kinderkrankenhaus) but they _________________________

(nicht überprüfen) the hospital rules first. So they ________________________ (organize O) their project better next time!
All of them are sure that they want to ________________________________ (so etwas wieder machen). They will keep _____________________ (versuchen) to help the community and they ____________________________ (freuen sich schon auf) it. On Saturday evening the students were happy but also tired and hungry. So some of the friends went to a take-away where they ____________ (machen) really nice burgers.

2. some, any, every, no and their compounds. Fill in the correct forms

Martha: Sally, where have you been? I've looked for you ____________________ but I couldn't find you _________________. I needed _______________ help with that poor calf.
Sally: Oh, I'm sorry. I was out with Rusty and I've found a great place for a picnic ______________________ near the river. Is there _______________ I can do for you now?
Martha: Yes, I just need _________________ help I can get at the moment. Can you go into the stable and give the calf _______________ milk, please? I have to prepare the barn for the square dance tonight. I hope ___________________ will enjoy it. But there's this unfriendly guest who is always angry about ___________________. ___________________ we can offer pleases him – he said there were flies _____________________. What does he think? It's a ranch, not a stylish hotel! ___________________ knows that!
Sally: Oh, yes, _______________ guest is better than Mr Holden. I hope he will leave soon and spend his vacation __________________ else next time! But before I go outside to give the calf its milk, could I have __________________ to drink first? I'm really thirsty!

III. Text Production

A reporter of the magazine „Great Vacations" is visiting the Lazy G because he wants to write an article about the Lazy G ranch. As Martha and Ed Gooch are busy at the moment, he interviews you, one of he guests at the Lazy G. Write down your answers to his questions in English (some ideas are given in German but you should add your own ideas, too). Use suitable (passende) adjectives and the new vocabulary. Write long sentences and connect your sentences

Reporter: Did the Goochs send you any information before you left for your vacation here? Did you know what special things to pack?
You: [Denke an die Prospekte und die Liste mit der benötigten Ausrüstung.]

____

____

____

Reporter: I know that the guests can take part in many aspects of ranch life. What have you done so far?
You: [Du hast schon am Viehtrieb und am Einfangen der Rinder mit dem Lasso teilgenommen. Du erklärst, was du genau gemacht hast und was Gäste, die da mitmachen wollen, können müssen.]

____

____

____

____

____

Reporter: That sounds really exciting! What do you usually do in the evenings - are there any organized activities?
You: [Du erzählst von Grillabenden (Forellen!) und Tanzabenden und warum es dir gefallen hat. Nur ein Gast hat sich beschwert, du bist aber nicht seiner Meinung.]

____

____

____

____

____

Reporter: What about the rooms and the horses? And what about Martha, Ed and Chuck? Would you recommend (empfehlen) the Lazy G to our readers?
You: [Du erklärst, warum die Zimmer eher einfach sind und erzählst von deinem Lieblingspferd. Du sagst etwas Nettes über die Goochs und Chuck und begründest, warum du die Ranch empfiehlst.]

Reporter: Thank you for your time. I'm sure our readers will want to visit the Lazy G, too!

Good luck !

Lösung: 4. Schulaufgabe aus dem Englischen

I. Vocabulary and grammar

1. Fill in suitable English words – sometimes the first letter is given, sometimes a German word is given. Be careful with the nouns (singular or plural?) and the verb forms (right tense). If there is a verb given with a P (for permission), an A (for ability) or an O (for obligation) behind it, it means that you must use this verb with the correct form of the auxiliary or its substitute

Cooper Middle School is in Denver, Colorado. It offers its 480 students a b*road* program of classes and a*ctivities*. The mission of Cooper Middle School is to keep up its long tradition of giving a good education to students from all *kinds* (Arten) of social backgrounds. The school's *aim* (Ziel) is to *prepare* (vorbereiten) its students for s*uccess* in college and life. To do that, the students always *take part in* (teilnehmen an) a very special day on the fourth Saturday in October. So, what projects *did* the students *do* (machen) last year? Of course, the students *had to talk* (talk O) about their plans first. They had a lot of ideas. Tina for example wanted to pick up *trash* (Abfall) in the park. But Sally said: "If we pick up trash, we *will need* (brauchen) a lot of bags. And it will be boring!" Tina answered: "Typical! If it *sounds like work* (sich nach Arbeit anhören) Sally isn't interested." But in the end they all found really good things to do.

José *didn't have to look* (not look O) far for his project. He and his father's band Corazón de Oro did some concerts and with the money they e*arned* they *were able to buy* (buy A) three small trees for the school. So the front of the school *will look* (aussehen) nice *when* (wenn) they have planted the trees. All the students *had to finish* (finish O) their projects on Saturday, only Bruce and Sven *were allowed to miss* (verpassen P) two classes on Monday because they *weren't able to go* (not go A) to the elementary schools on Saturday to deliver (= abgeben) their books. Sally and Tina made some cookies for the *children's hospital* (Kinderkrankenhaus) but they *didn't check* (nicht überprüfen) the hospital rules first. So they *will have to organize* (organize O) their project better next time!

All of them are sure that they want to *do something like that again* (so etwas wieder machen). They will keep *trying* (versuchen) to help the community and they *are looking forward to* (freuen sich schon auf) it. On Saturday evening the students were happy but also tired and hungry. So some of the friends went to a take-away where they *do* (machen) really nice burgers.

____/30

2. some, any, every, no and their compounds. Fill in the correct forms

Martha: Sally, where have you been? I've looked for you *everywhere* but I couldn't find you *anywhere*. I needed *some* help with that poor calf.

Sally: Oh, I'm sorry. I was out with Rusty and I've found a great place for a picnic *somewhere* near the river. Is there *anything* I can do for you now?

Martha: Yes, I just need *any* help I can get at the moment. Can you go into the stable and give the calf *some* milk, please? I have to prepare the barn for the square dance tonight. I hope *everybody* will enjoy it. But there's this unfriendly guest who is always angry about *something. Nothing* we can offer pleases him – he said there were flies *everywhere*. What does he think? It's a ranch, not a stylish hotel! *Everybody* knows that!

Sally: Oh, yes, *any* guest is better than Mr Holden. I hope he will leave soon and spend his vacation *somewhere* else next time! But before I go outside to give the calf its milk, could I have *something* to drink first? I'm really thirsty! ____/15

Tipps und Hinweise
Hier geht es um *some, someone, somebody, something, any, anybody, anything, every, everybody, everything, no, none, nobody, no-one* und *nothing.* In bejahten Sätzen verwendet man *some* mit seinen Zusammensetzungen. Denke daran, wenn das Verb im Satz verneint ist und bei einer Frage, brauchst du ein Wort mit *any*. Aufgepaßt! *Some* kann auch in Fragen auftauchen, wenn man eine positive Antwort erwartet oder wenn man etwas anbietet, und *any* in bejahten Aussagen, wenn es mit „jeder (beliebige)“ übersetzt wird.

III. Text Production

A reporter of the magazine „Great Vacations“ is visiting the Lazy G because he wants to write an article about the Lazy G ranch. As Martha and Ed Gooch are busy at the moment, he interviews you, one of he guests at the Lazy G. Write down your answers to his questions in English (some ideas are given in German but you should add your own ideas, too). Use suitable (passende) adjectives and the new vocabulary. Write long sentences and connect your sentences

Reporter: Did the Goochs send you any information before you left for your vacation here? Did you know what special things to pack?
You: [Denke an die Prospekte und die Liste mit der benötigten Ausrüstung.]

Yes, they did. They sent a gear list and they wrote that I need cowboy boots, thick socks, trousers, a jacket, a cowboy hat and a saddle if I prefer my own you can even get saddles in every size. They also sent some brochures with information about the activities and they wrote that they were looking forward to welcoming me at the Lazy G.

Reporter: I know that the guests can take part in many aspects of ranch life. What have you done so far?
You: [Du hast schon am Viehtrieb und am Einfangen der Rinder mit dem Lasso teilgenommen. Du erklärst, was du genau gemacht hast und was Gäste, die da mitmachen wollen, können müssen.]

I have just taken part even in branding and roping the cattle. As their guests we can take part in everything and we have to ride well. They teach you everything you need. You can enjoy all the activities they offer all the time.

Reporter: That sounds really exciting! What do you usually do in the evenings – are there any organized activities?
You: [Du erzählst von Grillabenden (Forellen!) und Tanzabenden und warum es dir gefallen hat. Nur ein Gast hat sich beschwert, du bist aber nicht seiner Meinung.]

Yes, there were BBQ evenings with trouts and dance evenings. It was very nice because dancing is my hobby. BBQ is very delicious especially when you grill the trout that you can catch in the river near the Lazy G. Only one guest wanted to complain about the horse he rode but I don't agree with him.

Reporter: What about the rooms and the horses? And what about Martha, Ed and Chuck? Would you recommend (empfehlen) the Lazy G to our readers?
You: [Du erklärst, warum die Zimmer eher einfach sind und erzählst von deinem Lieblingspferd. Du sagst etwas Nettes über die Goochs und Chuck und begründest, warum du die Ranch empfiehlst.]

The rooms are typical of a ranch that means stylish. My favourite horse is Rusty. I treat him very well and he's so cute. The Goochs and Chuck are very nice. They do everything for you. I would recommend the ranch because it's quite interesting to live there like a cowboy and there are many activities which you can take part in.

Reporter: Thank you for your time. I'm sure our readers will want to visit the Lazy G, too!

____/25

Total ____/60

Vom Consultant zum Bildungstrainer

„Wir bereiten speziell auf Schulaufgaben vor": Claus Arndt beim Nachhilfeunterricht mit Schülerin Kathi und seinem Sohn Alexander.

Claus Arndt (57) hat mit seiner Frau im eigenen Haus ein Lernstudio eröffnet

Claus Arndt hat schon immer gerne unterrichtet. Dass der Dipl.-Mathematiker dieses Hobby irgendwann zum Beruf machen würde, war aber alles andere als vorhersehbar.

Seit den 80er Jahren hat der Vater zweier Söhne als Software-Ingenieur und Presales-Consultant gearbeitet, zuletzt 13 Jahre im selben Unternehmen. Doch 2004 war damit Schluss: „Die Firma hat mit einem Mal großflächig Personal abgespeckt", erzählt der Waldtruderinger. „Wer gehen wollte, konnte gehen". Die Entscheidung fiel Arndt leicht, auch weil er eine Abfindung erhielt. Was er damit anfangen würde, darüber muss er nicht lange grübeln. „Ich hatte schon als Student Repetitorien für BWL-Studenten gehalten und mochte die Arbeit immer gerne."

Mit seiner Frau Monika, Autorin und Übersetzerin, entschied er sich, im Keller ihres Hauses ein Nachhilfestudio zu eröffnen und selbst als **Bildungstrainer** zu arbeiten. „Wir hatten schon immer im Hinterkopf, dass hier in Waldtrudering die Klientel dafür da ist", sagt Arndt. Denn Nachhilfe ist ein Luxus.

Um sich vorzubereiten, heuerte Arndt ein Jahr als Aushilfslehrer für Mathematik an, zunächst in der Realschule Dachau, später im Heinrich-Heine-Gymnasium.

Mittlerweile hat das **Durchblicker Lernstudio Arndt** einen festen Stamm von rund 25 Schülern, die regelmäßig kommen. Eine Stunde Bildungstraining kostet bis zu 50 Euro. „Es war die beste Idee, mich selbständig zu machen", sagt Arndt. „Nur eines bereue ich: Dass ich es nicht früher gemacht habe."

Arndt unterrichtet die Nachhilfeschüler in Mathematik, seine Frau in Englisch, Deutsch und Französisch. Wenn die Nachfrage groß genug ist, zum Beispiel zum Schuljahresende hin, helfen weitere Nachhilfelehrer mit aus.

„Wichtig für den Erfolg ist, dass wir die Wünsche unserer Kunden erfüllen." Dazu gehören Crashkurse oder Intensivtraining. Außerdem setzt Arndt auf Werbung: Zuletzt hat er einen Werbefilm für die Kinoleinwand in Auftrag gegeben.

„Meine Spezialität ist, die Schüler direkt auf die Schulaufgaben vorzubereiten", sagt der 57-Jährige. Passend dazu bringen er und seine Frau im Eigenverlag Bücher heraus, in denen sie modifizierte Schulaufgaben und deren ausführliche Lösungen besprechen. „Zu jeder Schulaufgabe gebe ich eine persönliche Einschätzung und kennzeichne Aufgaben, die sich als G8-Standard herauskristallisiert haben."

Erst vor kurzem hat sich eine Mutter in einem Brief bedankt: „Meine Tochter kapiert Mathe am besten, wenn Sie es ihr vor den Schulaufgaben erklären."

Bericht von Vanessa Assmann in der Münchner Abendzeitung vom 15.3.2011

Ich wollte Ihnen mitteilen, dass ich in der Mathe-Schulaufgabe eine 1 habe. Ich habe die Aufgaben vor der Schulaufgabe alle durchgerechnet und fühlte mich dadurch fit und sicher.

Mit den Schulaufgaben von bayerischen Gymnasien Französisch bin ich sehr gut vorbereitet für die Schulaufgabe.

Physik und Chemie sind so gut erklärt, dass ich es in den Schulaufgaben einfach umsetzen kann.

Dank Ihrer Bücher und mit dem Bayerischen Mathematik-Test (BMT) habe ich die 10. Klasse in Mathematik und damit die Mittlere Reife geschafft.

Die Hinweise zu den Matheaufgaben haben meinem Sohn soviel Selbstbewusstsein gegeben, dass er in seiner Schulaufgabe die Note 1 geschrieben hat.

So gute Erklärungen und Tipps hatte ich noch nie. Die Hinweise in den ausführlichen Lösungen sind die absoluten Insidertipps! Damit weiß ich endlich, was dran kommt.

VOLLTREFFER !!!
3 Aufgaben in meiner Schulaufgabe waren genau wie die aus Ihrem Buch. Danke!

Den besten Mathelehrer der Welt habe ich die Note 1 im Abitur zu verdanken.

Super eine 2 in Englisch! Die Schulaufgaben von bayerischen Gymnasien Englisch haben mir sehr geholfen.

Mein Sohn Leander hat sich schon letztes Jahr ausschließlich mit Ihren Heften auf seine Schulaufgaben in Mathe und Englisch vorbereitet, was uns zu einem insgesamt recht entspannten ersten Schuljahr im Gymnasium verholfen hat. Wir erleben Ihre Hefte als echte Unterstützung!

Englisch 6

ISBN: 978-3-00-034521-0

9 783000 345210

€ 14,95 (D) € 15,40 (A)